Wicca FOR
Everyday Life

Wicca FOR Everyday Life

CELTIC SPELLS, CHANTS, AND RITUALS FOR BUSY WITCHES

Silja

CICO BOOKS

Dedicated to my three wonderful, magical children and all the
spiritual people who keep the hope alive in dark times.

Published in 2025 by CICO Books
An imprint of Ryland Peters & Small Ltd
20–21 Jockey's Fields   1452 Davis Bugg Road
London WC1R 4BW   Warrenton, NC 27589
www.rylandpeters.com
Email: euregulations@rylandpeters.com

10 9 8 7 6 5 4 3 2 1

A CIP record for this book is available from the
British Library.
US Library of Congress CIP data has been applied for.

ISBN: 978-1-80065-431-0

Printed in China

Illustrator: Hannah Davies
Commissioning editor: Kristine Pidkameny
Editors: Kristy Richardson and Imogen Valler-Miles
Senior designer: Emily Breen
Art director: Sally Powell
Creative director: Leslie Harrington
Production manager: Gordana Simakovic
Head of production: Patricia Harrington
Publishing manager: Carmel Edmonds

The authorised representative in the EEA is
Authorised Rep Compliance Ltd.,
Ground Floor. 71 Lower Baggot Street,
Dublin, D01 P593, Ireland
www.arccompliance.com

Safety note:
Neither the author nor the publisher can be held responsible
for any claim arising out of the general information and
practices provided in this book. Please note that while the
use of essential oils, herbs, incense, and particular practices
refer to healing benefits, they are not intended to replace
diagnosis of illness or ailments, or healing or medicine.
Always consult your doctor or other health professional in
the case of illness. Essential oils are very powerful and
potentially toxic if used too liberally. Please follow the advice
given on the label and never use the oils neat on bare skin,
or if pregnant. The safe and proper use of candles is the sole
responsibility of the person using them. Do not leave a
burning candle unattended. Never burn a candle on or near
anything that might catch fire. Keep candles out of the reach
of children and pets.

Contents

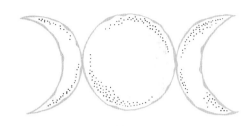

Introduction

Wicca can easily be incorporated into our everyday lives. The great thing about Wicca, and magic in general, is that it is so adaptable. I hope this fact is reflected in this book, which is suitable for busy witches as well as those who just want to dip their toes into magical practices.

WHAT IS WICCA?

"Pagan," "Wiccan," and "witch" are often used interchangeably, but the terms have very different meanings. First of all, witchcraft is not a religion. As the name implies, it's a craft that involves magic, but that also works with the power of herbs and crystals, alternative medicine, astrology, mythology, and various methods of fortune-telling.

You do not have to be a Pagan to be a witch. I know Jewish, Christian, and even atheist witches! Paganism is an umbrella term for lots of different earth-based spiritualities and religions—many, but not all, of them stemming from pre-Christian beliefs. The main ones are Wicca, Druidism, Asatru, Voodoo, Shamanism, and Hedgewitchery. By far the most well-known and popular of these Pagan paths is Wicca.

Many traditions have evolved within Wicca, based on varying practices and revering different cultural deities, from Celtic to ancient Egyptian. However, these generally involve a coven led by a high priestess, and various stages of initiation. Spiritual gatherings are called Esbats (for Full Moon rituals) and Sabbats (for larger festivals), and while they change with the seasons, they are usually quite similar each time.

Through the years, my witchy practices have changed, going from eclectic Wicca where I dabbled in a bit of everything, through traditional Alexandrian Wicca, to Celtic Wicca when I started my own coven. After I had my kids, I simply didn't have much time for elaborate rituals and bimonthly coven meetups anymore, so I went back to a more eclectic, Hedgewitchery type of witchcraft, albeit still with Celtic Wiccan roots.

Many people, when they first become interested in Wicca and witchcraft, are looking to join a coven right away. However, that is the wrong time to join a magical group. Of course, I am not saying that joining a coven is a bad thing—I have run one for years—but first, you should explore by yourself, both intellectually and spiritually, so that you can do your magic and worship exactly when and how you want, and learn which tradition of Wicca and which pantheon of deities works for you.

There are guidelines when it comes to morals and practice, of course, and certain things work better for some people than others, but Wicca is a wonderfully changeable religion. It can change with your views, your experience, the amount of time and money or supplies you have to devote to it, and anything else that influences your life.

WICCAN ETHICS

Wicca doesn't have a bible or a set of ten commandments, but that doesn't mean a lack of values and ethics—quite the opposite! Wicca has two main ethical guidelines for both performing magic and living spiritually.

AND IT HARM NONE, DO AS THOU WILT

This is the basic Wiccan moral standpoint. At first glance, this seems pretty easy: do as you wish, as long as you don't cause harm. But it can be a little more complicated than just making sure that the herb you are going to use isn't poisonous! "And it harm none" refers not only to other people, but also to yourself, animals, plants, and the Earth herself. We are all connected to each other—spiritually, ecologically, and physically —and we must carefully weigh our actions with their consequences.

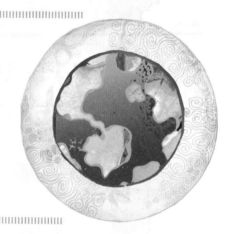

LEST IN THY SELF-DEFENSE IT BE, EVER MIND THE RULE OF THREE

This one is a little easier. Just think of karma, or of reaping what you sow. Wiccans believe that what you do comes back to you threefold, so if you send out bad energy in the form of a spell or action, not only does it backfire on you, but you also suffer three times the consequence! If you have been deliberately harmed by someone, rest assured they will suffer the consequences, even if they are not immediately obvious.

CELTIC WICCA

The Celtic tradition my coven practiced, and that I still mostly follow, is based on the practices of pre-Christian Celtic Europe (and Ireland—technically not Celtic but still part of the culture). This is with the acknowledgment that there are many things from those days that we do not truly know about or are unsuitable for modern worship. Much of the Celtic tradition is adaptable to the season and your tastes and beliefs—I add Native American deities and herbs when in the US—as well as how much time you have for magic on a particular day or for a particular goal. This tradition is extremely earth- and nature-based, because most ancient Celts were farmers and had to be mindful of Mother Nature.

There are many symbols associated with Celtic Wicca. Celtic symbols are found on ancient monuments such as Newgrange, in Ireland, and Stonehenge, in England. While they are pretty decorations, they also have powerful meanings and are still in use today—they are sometimes used as part of maps to signify burial mounds and fairy forts.

Some of the Celtic symbols you will see throughout this book are:

• **The Tree of Life**, which is a symbol of strength and resilience, and the balance of Mother Earth (in the roots) and Father Sky (in the branches).

• **The Triquetra or Trinity Knot**, which is thought to be the oldest spiritual symbol, and represents the belief that everything important comes in three. This was later adopted by Christianity with the Father, Son, and Holy Ghost.

• **The Triple Spiral or Triskele**, which also symbolizes that everything good comes in threes, as well as symbolizing harmony.

• **The Shield Knot**, which signifies confidence, protection, and unity.

• **The Wheel**, which represents the solar calendar and the eight most important Celtic Wiccan festivals.

• **The Double Spiral**, which symbolizes the perfect balance needed in the world—between night and day, male and female, and God and Goddess.

MAGIC AND MYTHOLOGY

The world is full of wonderful mythological stories, and
I encourage all students of Wicca and witchcraft to read the
mythology of their own ancestors, of where they live, and of any
other cultures that they feel drawn to (you may be drawn to them
due to past lives there). While Wicca is a modern religion—less
than one hundred years old—mythology can teach us about
ethics, history, emotions, and how to cope with difficult
situations, plus those stories are plainly a good read!

Many mythological stories involve witches and magicians
(just think of Merlin!), so you can learn about magical
people and places too. But mythology can also be used
more directly in spells and rituals. Many stories mention
herbs, colors, or crystals used in magic, such as the story
of Dian Cécht, the old Irish healing god, who used magical
healing water from holy springs mixed with feverfew to heal the
Tuatha Dé Danann people after battles. Nowadays, these springs
are still used by Catholics and Wiccans in Ireland to drink from when
they are ill, and feverfew is known as a healing herb among alternative
medical practitioners and witches alike.

THE THEORY OF HOW MAGIC WORKS

Because magic only changes probability, it means you won't be
100 percent successful. It doesn't matter whether the magic you do is
a quick chant while waiting for an appointment, or an elaborate ritual
with an experienced coven—if you do a spell to win the lottery, even if your
chances double, the percentage chance of winning is still tiny. But if you are
one of three people up for a promotion and you do a spell to get the job, then
doubling your chances means you have a very good shot at that promotion!
Magic essentially works with the energy of the universe to change probability.
The chanting, herbs, visualization, and crystals help with that because they
have their own magical energies, but you are the main part.

MAGICAL SUPPLIES

Magic can be done with nothing other than your body and mind.
You are the magical energy that makes things happen with your intent.
A lot of quick and simple magical practices involve visualizations (also
known as manifestations), chanting (you can even do this quietly in your
mind if you are with unsupportive family or in public), or dancing!

But there are certainly some supplies that help with your quick magic,
and they do not have to be expensive things from the occult store.

• **Clothing:** Because colors play a part in magic, I find it helpful to have
clothes in most major colors to hand. I don't mean a witchy robe—just
items such as a yellow skirt when I want to encourage friendships, blue
jeans when I need to heal, a red blouse to increase passion, or a black
jacket to absorb negative energy.

• **Herbs:** Much can be done with the herbs that most of us have at home
for cooking. You can use them intentionally in the kitchen with magic in
mind (more on this in Chapter 1), but also outside of food—such as rolling
a candle in a herb before lighting it, sprinkling some in a bath, or adding
a sprig of lavender to a beautifully wrapped gift.

• **Crystals:** Gems and crystals are from Mother Earth and thus are
inherently magical. Having some basic crystals like clear quartz, rose
quartz, and amethyst around will help with quick magic spells.

CHAPTER 1

Witchery in the Home and Garden

From your backyard to your front door, you can sprinkle
a little Wiccan magic all around your home to keep
everything and everyone inside it happy, healthy,
and well protected.

Your magical home

Your home should feel like a haven of acceptance. Try these tips to keep your abode magically safe and peaceful, as well as to add some extra positive energy.

RESTORING PEACEFUL ENERGY

Sometimes the atmosphere in our homes can turn sour. After a fight, or a visit from the in-laws you don't get along with, or when moving into a new home, cleanse your home from negative energy with these simple tricks.

• For every room in your home, cut a lemon into quarters and place in all four corners of the room. While you do this, say: "The bitterness of lemon, like negativity's venom, fly away, be now gone, lemon's yellow shine, like the sun!" Throw them away after a few days, along with any negative energy they have soaked up.

• Place a clear crystal wrapped in a yellow cloth in the room (you can hide it if you wish, such as under the bed or in a plant pot), so the room will feel friendly and have a strong positive energy.

• Smudging can help, too. Buy smudge sticks, dry your own sage, or use sage essential oil with water in a spray bottle. Make sure to have the windows open while smudging so the smoke can leave —and any negative energy with it!

• Wash the floors, windows, and door frames with spring water or water from a stream, to which you've added a few drops of geranium and lemongrass essential oils. This will remove negativity, stress, and any bad energy.

• For positivity, bless your home with rose water sprinkled around each room in a clockwise direction.

• Cleanse your home with sound. Ring a pleasant-sounding bell while walking around each room in a clockwise direction.

• Consider strategic planting. A lovely, prickly holly bush outside your house should be quite a deterrent to negativity and is a symbol of a witch's power. Alternatively, place a cactus close to your front door.

PRACTICAL MAGIC **PROTECTION POTION**

Create a magic mixture to protect your home from nasty neighbors and break-ins. You will need coarse salt, which represents peace and the protection of Mother Earth, black pepper to absorb negativity, vinegar to cleanse the mind and emotions, and clove oil (or whole cloves, crushed) to ward off gossip and bad energy.

1 Mix the coarse salt, black pepper, and vinegar together and add a few drops of clove oil (or crushed whole cloves).

2 Coat your fence posts and threshold with the mixture, preferably on a waning moon, which symbolizes the lessening of the bad people's power.

3 Repeat this once a week or after heavy rains.

BESOM BLESSINGS

When keeping a home comfy, the witch's broom comes into its own. Try to make sure your broom is made from natural materials, with a wooden handle and a reed brush (rather than plastic). Leave it out in the moonlight to be blessed by the Goddess, and in sunlight to be blessed by the God. Decorate it in a way that attracts the things you want or dispels the things you don't (see box below). While you use the broom, sweep it clockwise to bring more of something (such as financial success) or counterclockwise to lessen something (such as a sickness). Keep it by the front door when not in use.

ADORN YOUR BROOM

GREEN RIBBON: To bring financial success to those living in the home.

YELLOW LEAVES: To invite friendly neighbors.

BLUE FLOWERS: To heal sickness in the home.

WINDOWS AND DOORS

Pay special attention to the front door and windows of your home. These entryways and exits are where people, as well as positive and negative energies, can flow in and out.

• Hang cut-glass crystals in the windows. They will make rainbow patterns on the walls that can attract fairies.

• Place green objects by your front door to keep your home and its inhabitants flourishing financially. For example, plant a bush just outside, place a leafy green plant on a shelf in the entrance hall, or paint your front door green.

• Keep three copper coins under your front doormat to draw money into the home.

• Keep windows and doors open when you can so that Mother Nature can blow the wind through to bring change and help remove negativity or bad memories.

SOAP SORCERY

I recommend having more than one type of soap on the go for washing dishes, your hands, or your clothes. I like to switch soap scents and colors depending on what I am trying to magically attract.

BASIL AND LEMONGRASS HAND SOAP: Attracts money.

LAVENDER-SCENTED DETERGENT: Use for bed linen and pajamas to bring a good night's sleep.

LEMON-SCENTED DISHWASHING LIQUID: Fosters friendships and gets rid of negativity.

PURPLE HAND SOAP: Strengthens occult powers and knowledge—ideal for cleaning up before reading tarot cards or doing a ritual.

CONSIDER THE FURNITURE

Think about the furnishings in your home and how they can impact your life. It's totally okay to buy whatever you can afford or works best for you. While color can encourage love, calmness, healing, or money, do not feel that everything in your home needs to be a "magical color." For example, I have lots of pets, so our living room furniture is generally gray-brown or patterned to hide all the fur!

• It's easy to "witchify" furniture with a colorful blanket or a pillow with a pentagram embroidered on it.

• If you want your family to communicate better, get an L-shaped sofa, rather than one long one, or arrange several comfy chairs in a U-shape.

• Sneak magical ingredients into or under your furniture—place a tiger's eye stone in the drawer of your child's homework desk to encourage studying and the retention of knowledge.

• If illness, either mental or physical, is an issue for you or your family, consider incorporating calm and healing blue into your home, such as blue cookware or spatulas, blue bed linen, or a blue shower curtain or soap holder.

• House fairies can be mischievous. It's not a bad idea to bribe them with a piece of chocolate or a sprinkle of sugar on a pretty plate or in a bowl of marbles. You could also keep a cute fairy statue or drawing near your washing machine to help you stop losing single socks!

PRACTICAL MAGIC **ADAPTABLE ALTARS**

It's great to have a dedicated space for magic. But it doesn't need to be a whole room or a massive, permanent altar! Your altar can be a windowsill, mantelpiece, or even a space on your bookshelf. If you don't have much space, or need to stay covert about your witchiness, a portable altar it is!

1 Paint or embroider a pentagram onto a white cloth.

2 Wrap your witchy supplies up in the cloth and stash it in a drawer or under your bed when not in use.

3 Bring it out whenever you need to practice. You can even take it outside to practice in a park or in the forest!

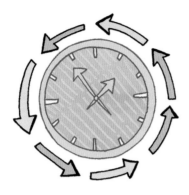

Your magical kitchen

The kitchen is the heart of the home, where food and conversation are shared. Any ingredient used for cooking can be magical, but some pack a particular magical punch.

STIRRING UP MAGIC

The easiest way to incorporate magic while in the kitchen is by paying attention to how you stir your food and drinks while cooking. Stirring clockwise (deosil) will increase positive outcomes while stirring counterclockwise (widdershins) will decrease negative ones. While you stir, think about the issue that is concerning you.

STORAGE TIPS

KNIVES AND SCISSORS: If it is safe to do so, leave knives and scissors out to encourage you to cut out bad people or habits.

POTS AND PANS: Store pots and pans upside down to let bad luck fall out of your life.

JARS, CUPBOARDS, AND DRAWERS: Make sure you always close jars, cupboards, and drawers to keep good fortune with you.

EGGS

Eggs are a symbol of eternal life and rebirth, as well as the goddess Eostre. They are a powerful ingredient to keep in the kitchen.

• If you find an egg with two yolks, it means you'll have good luck for the rest of the year!

• White eggs stand for peace and the Moon Goddess. As you stir them clockwise into other food ingredients, say: "Eggs bring us peace, trouble and strife will now cease!"

• Brown eggs represent prosperity and Mother Earth. When cooking with brown eggs, stir them clockwise and say:

"As of these eggs we feed, may we have all the money we need!"

• Painting eggs is not just for Easter. Paint them with runes in the color of something you want to attract, such as an orange arrow pointing upward for justice.

• Gain the energy of the Sun God by making a fried egg. The yolk in the middle symbolizes the Sun God, and the white around it represents pure energy.

POTATOES

Potatoes are a staple part of many meals. They bring you closer to Mother Nature due to their brown color, and because they are grown in the earth.

To achieve a goal—anything from losing weight to gaining a promotion or finding a new friend—cut a potato in two, then carve a symbol of what you desire inside. (For example, this could be the number of pounds you want to lose, a coin to represent a promotion, or a stick figure to symbolize a new friend.) Put the potato back together and bake or microwave it. Eat it with sour cream or a white cheese (white to symbolize the purity of your intention and magical energy).

PUMPKINS

Pumpkins are not just for Halloween. Gourds of all kinds have a variety
of uses and are an essential ingredient for any witch's kitchen.

• A simple fortune-telling method is to throw a handful of pumpkin seeds in the air while thinking about an issue or question you have. Interpret the shape they make when they land.

• If you are in a dispute, such as with a work colleague, or you need justice in a court or custody case, make and eat a dish using pumpkin—cookies or shortbread are especially good! As you prepare it, stir counterclockwise and chant: "Remove the disguise, stop the obstacles and lies!" Then stir clockwise and chant: "Justice I need, by pumpkin flesh and pumpkin seed." If possible, offer the other party some of the food too.

PRACTICAL MAGIC **PUMPKIN CARVING**

This simple ritual can help you to get in touch with departed loved ones, or ancestors from far in the past.

1 Hollow out a pumpkin (either in a plain shape or with a friendly face).

2 Light a black candle and place it inside the pumpkin.

3 Place a photo of the person (or their name written on a piece of paper) in front of the pumpkin. Close your eyes and think about this person. Why do you want to get in touch with them?

4 Open your eyes and look to the flame of the candle for a message. For example, the flame may look like a heart because the person still loves you from beyond, or it may flicker toward a side of the house they want you to do something in. The flame may just extinguish if the departed would prefer that you forget them.

5 If you can't see a message in the flame, the person may come to you in a dream that night.

CAULIFLOWER

Cauliflower is not only a versatile food that can be roasted, boiled, riced, or used as a pizza crust, but it is also a versatile magical ingredient due to its white color, which symbolizes peace, pure energy, and fresh starts.

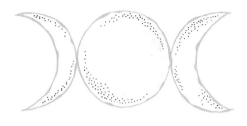

• To add power and pure energy to any ritual or spell, sprinkle some riced or finely cut cauliflower in a pentagram shape on your altar or around the magical object (such as tarot cards or quartz point) you are empowering.

• If you need more peace to meditate, or to be more creative, make a cauliflower dish. While cooking, stir it counterclockwise. Imagine the bad energy and negative people going away with the steam. Then, stir clockwise. Imagine the Moon Goddess' energy and the creativity of the universe entering the dish. The dish will nourish the mind and body of anyone who eats it.

• To find out how to perform a divination with cauliflower, see page 125.

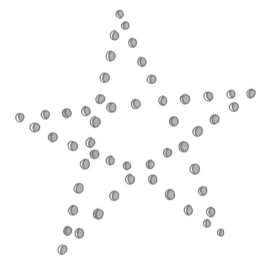

RASPBERRIES

In witchcraft, raspberries are associated with romantic love due to their pink color, and protection due to their prickly stems, as well as being connected with intuition, kindness, and motherhood. To add a little magic to a snack or dessert, make filled raspberries! Fill them with cream (white for pure energy and peace), custard (yellow for friendship), or chocolate (brown for grounding).

PEARS

If people who mean you ill need to enter your home or office, place a branch of a pear tree on the threshold for them to step over. This will neutralize any negativity. You can also eat a pear, or make a pear dish to share with them, to make them more positive toward you.

SUGAR

Sugar is not used in magical spells very much, but in witchcraft it represents the Triple Goddess (Maiden, Mother, and Crone) and the Moon Goddess, due to its brilliant white color. Unrefined or brown sugar symbolizes the Earth Goddess. You can find your inner goddess and manifest her beauty by making or buying a sugar scrub and rubbing it into your skin clockwise while chanting:

A Goddess is in me,

Today, everyone will see!

Beautiful and strong,

They will know before long.

PRACTICAL MAGIC **SUGAR SORCERY**

Do you need to let go of a bad habit, or a person who isn't good for you?

1 Sit quietly and rub some lemon on your lips while you think of the bad things that the situation or relationship has caused.

2 When you are ready, say goodbye to the bad habit or person in your mind and rub some sugar onto your lips to symbolize the sweetness of life without them.

3 Whenever you long for the bad habit or person, repeat step 2 until the moment passes.

CINNAMON

Are you coming out of a bad relationship or job, or just need a change? These three ways with cinnamon will bring energy, passion, and spice to your life.

• To gain more energy, leave a clear quartz in a bag of cinnamon, or rub it with cinnamon oil while chanting: "Energy I need, my passions I'll feed, great ideas I'll seed, as I will it, so mote it be!"

• Draw a warm bath and stir in a generous tablespoon of cinnamon. First stir counterclockwise and visualize the bad things in your life disappearing, then stir clockwise and imagine new energy and passion coming into your life. You can do this with a drink, too, by adding a small teaspoon of cinnamon to hot water with lemon.

• To spice up your sex life, make a red dish using cinnamon, such as a tomato sauce or a cinnamon cake with strawberries on top. As you cook, chant nine times: "Eros and Aphrodite, come to us, bring us fun, love, and lust!"

CUMIN

There are several ways you can incorporate cumin into your magic.

• To strengthen and improve yourself as a person, add cumin to a favorite dish. Stir counterclockwise while thinking of the negative qualities and features you want to lessen, then clockwise while thinking about the positive qualities that you want to strengthen or acquire.

• To help understand another's point of view (when discussing the future with your partner or during business negotiations), chew five cumin seeds immediately before the meeting while chanting: "Lord and Lady help me understand, so happily together we may band, everyone shall be content, with the empathy you sent!" (You can repeat this quietly in your head during the meeting if necessary.)

• If you cannot get over someone or need help moving past a situation, grind some cumin and add it to almond oil (almonds for happiness and good luck). Massage a little oil into your skin every morning.

• Add some cumin to things you really don't want to lose.

• Sprinkle ground cumin, black pepper, and salt clockwise around the house to protect it from bad influences and theft.

SAFFRON

Associated with prediction and foretelling, just three strands of this powerful spice can bring a positive future. Hold the strands to your heart (so it may be guided to a loving future) and then to your forehead (so your third eye may be opened to see the future). After this, place one of the strands of saffron in your wallet—or another place where you keep your money—for a prosperous future; one on the left side of your body to improve your intuition; and chew one slowly to have your whole body and being guided by the Gods and Goddesses.

PRACTICAL MAGIC **SAFFRON DIVINATION**

Saffron is a useful spice for those who wish to see the future, have a prophetic dream, or gain more clarity and insight during divinations like reading tea leaves or tarot cards.

1 Before beginning a divination, chew a single strand of saffron.

2 Rub some saffron into a purple candle.

3 Chant nine times: "The future will become clear, things that are far and near, God and Goddess let me view, things that I never knew!"

4 Light the candle and stare into it while thinking of a particular issue or future event you want clarity on.

5 As you look into the candle flame, you may see the face of a person who can help. If you do not see anything, then you may dream about it that night. If the flame is very calm, so too will be the minds and emotions of the people involved.

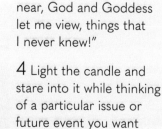

GINGER

Ginger can increase the energy of any magic, and ginger root in particular can be used to draw positive things to you.

• If you need money, cut a ginger root horizontally to make coin-like slices, and add them to your wallet. Replace them when they start to look shriveled.

• To grant more energy to a home's inhabitants, add some ginger essential oil to your floor and window washes.

• To increase the energy of your magic, eat some candied ginger or a dish with ginger root before doing a ritual.

• Rub your magical objects—from your wand or pentagram jewelry to tarot cards or your stash of colored candles—with a freshly cut ginger root to add extra magical power.

To draw romance or a significant other into your life, consider what qualities you are looking for in a partner. Carve words or symbols for those things into a ginger root—for example, a house for someone who has their own home, a baby stick figure if you want children soon, or the minimum height of your prospective partner. Leave it on your altar or a windowsill until you find that person. While you carve, chant:

Love and passion come to me,
A good partner I will soon see!
God and Goddess help me find,
A mate with whom my life to bind.

NUTMEG

Two trees are required to produce nutmeg, one male and one female. In witchcraft, this symbolizes the need for balance and helping each other. The female tree carries the egg-shaped nutmeg, symbolizing fertility and nourishment. Nutmeg can be used to find stability in this topsy-turvy world, from keeping a financial situation stable to keeping yourself and others calm in stressful or emotional situations.

• Sprinkle nutmeg in a pentagram shape on warm milk or a dish before eating. Milk works especially well because of the white color, representing peace.

• A whole nutmeg carried in a pocket to the left side of your body brings luck and safe travels; carried on the right, it strengthens people's trust in you and helps your plans and dreams stay realistic.

• To encourage calm collaboration between family members or colleagues, rub nutmeg on the dining or meeting room table.

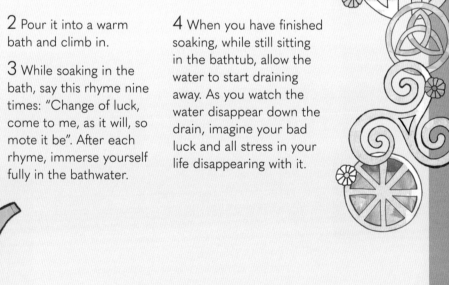

PRACTICAL MAGIC **NUTMEG BATH**

Change your luck with this bathtime ritual using nutmeg.

1 Brew up a teapot using five teaspoons of nutmeg and one cup of boiling water.

2 Pour it into a warm bath and climb in.

3 While soaking in the bath, say this rhyme nine times: "Change of luck, come to me, as it will, so mote it be". After each rhyme, immerse yourself fully in the bathwater.

4 When you have finished soaking, while still sitting in the bathtub, allow the water to start draining away. As you watch the water disappear down the drain, imagine your bad luck and all stress in your life disappearing with it.

PEPPER

Burning red peppercorns is considered a deterrent against supernatural beings, especially werewolves and vampires, and according to mythology can also help expel demons. While demons are not usually an issue in present times, pepper offers many protective qualities for the modern witch.

• If you have a relative or acquaintance visiting who you think means you ill, before they arrive, burn red peppercorns in your fireplace, or roast some in a frying pan, to help ward off the evil eye.

• Sprinkle burnt red peppercorns under your bed to ward off nightmares.

• If you want a fun night with your partner, sprinkle black and red pepper over food while chanting: "Love and passion we will find, with these words this spell I bind!"

• If you are struggling with jealousy, either of your own or from others, sprinkle a pinch of black pepper on your head before you leave your home in the morning. As the pepper falls to the ground, visualize the jealous thoughts in your head or negative opinions of others falling away and being absorbed by Mother Nature.

• When sprinkling pepper around you or on your altar, choose an appropriate color of pepper to add more magical energy to any ritual or spell (see box below).

PEPPERCORN COLORS

WHITE: For energy and peace.

RED: For passion and virility.

PINK: For romantic love.

BLACK: For solving conflict and banishing negativity. Also an aphrodisiac.

GREEN: For financial and business success.

GARLIC

Garlic is a potent protection herb that can ward off more than just vampires.

• Add garlic to foods to protect you and your family magically as well as to boost your immune system. Choose white garlic for general magic—as white gives energy to any magic and represents peace—or purple garlic for occult knowledge and wisdom.

• Add garlic bulbs to a wreath for your front door to ward off illness and negativity.

• Place a clove of garlic on the outside of every windowsill and doorway to stop negative energy and people (including thieves and gossips) from entering.

Is there someone in your life—maybe a family member, co-worker, or acquaintance—who just leaves you feeling drained after talking to them? They may be a psychic vampire: someone who leeches energy and positivity from others, sometimes knowingly but often subconsciously. To protect yourself, visualize yourself in the middle of a bulb of garlic, happy, and full of energy before meeting such a person.

To get in touch with the goddess Hecate (patron deity of witches), or the ghosts or spirits of your ancestors, rub a black or purple candle with garlic oil, light it, and chant:

Goddess Hecate [or name of your ancestor], come to me,

Show me the way, let me see!

Your protection and guidance I seek,

Keep me honest and strong, yet meek.

Ask the goddess or your ancestor any questions you may have, then watch the candle flame and interpret its shape or movement to find your answers.

WALNUTS

Walnuts can help to ground you. After an exciting or stressful time, or after doing magic or talking to spirits and ancestors, try holding a piece of walnut wood (such as a piece of walnut furniture), or eating a few walnuts. To get in touch with spirits, especially nature spirits in your area, place a circle of walnuts around you. Sit comfortably, slow your breathing, and chant this slowly seven times:

Spirits, come to me,

Nature energy, let me see,

What is the right way,

What is the right thing to say?

PRACTICAL MAGIC **WITCHCRAFT WITH WALNUT**

Try the following spell for growth or to satisfy your needs.

1 Write what you need on a small piece of paper. This could be a specific amount of money, emotional health in your relationship, or finding a witchy coven for spiritual growth.

2 Open a walnut gently into two halves and place the piece of paper inside.

3 Drip some green wax (for abundance) onto the edge of both halves and close the walnut quickly so the wax seals it.

4 Bury the walnut in a favorite spot outside and let Mother Earth transform your wish into reality.

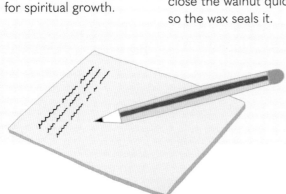

ALMONDS

The word almond comes from the Greek *amygdalus*—the ancient Greek name of the goddess Cybele, the Great Mother Goddess. Show gratitude for the blessings the God and Goddess have brought you, and request their blessing and protection on future projects with the following spells.

• Eat something with almonds in it (at dusk for the Goddess and at dawn for the God) while saying: "Lord and Lady I thank thee, for the blessings you have given me, I ask for your protection, please show me the right direction!"

• If you need guidance from the deities, create a pentagram with almonds on your altar and meditate about the issue.

• Scatter almonds on your nightstand and ask the deities for dreams about the issue.

• Eating some almonds before reading tarot cards or other fortune-telling can help make the results clearer.

• Bring yourself luck by carrying five almonds (preferably in their shell to also bring protection) on your left-hand side.

CHOCOLATE AND CACAO

Its brown color makes chocolate a good food to use in earth-based or grounding spells as well as rituals that get you closer to the Earth Goddess, and to loving yourself exactly as you are.

• Make a good-quality hot chocolate with cinnamon for you and your partner, or feed each other good-quality dark chocolate, before having fun in the bedroom.

• If you have been having doubts about your past actions or future path in life, place a cacao bean under your pillow before going to sleep. Ask the goddess Ixcacao to help you accept and love yourself as you are. Chant the following to yourself as you fall asleep: "I feel it! I heal it! You may not be perfect, but you are the best you can be!"

• To help toward your goal, be that in a career, becoming or being a better parent, or following your artistic dreams, sit comfortably, and place a few raw cacao nibs in your mouth. Visualize yourself as the best you can be, accepting of your flaws and happy with yourself.

• Place a few cacao nibs in the bottom of a healthy potted plant to symbolize your connection with nature and your emotional and mental health.

Your magical garden

Your magical garden can be anything from a box on the windowsill to a ten-acre property with your own fairy fort and forest.

HOW DOES YOUR GARDEN GROW?

Your garden should be a space where you can sit and enjoy Mother Nature. But it is also a good idea for it to include a nice mix of vegetables, fruits, and herbs that you can use as both food and magical ingredients. The magical tips and tricks below will help both you and your garden to flourish and thrive:

• To help your plants grow, cup your hands around the pot or main stem of the plant. Blow gently on it and say: "This is the breath of life. It will infuse this plant with healthy energy so it may thrive!"

• Keep the Moon Goddess in mind. Plant root vegetables, and other plants that grow downward, during a waning moon. Prune and cut plants during a waning or new moon. Plants or flowers that grow upward, such as trees, should be planted during a waxing moon (or during a full moon, if the flowers are the most important part of the plant).

• Hang up a hammock or get a comfy outdoor lounger in colors that appeal to you and help your current magical goals, such as purple to deepen your magical knowledge. Try yellow cushions to improve friendships with people coming to visit.

• A water feature—such as a birdbath, fountain, or little pond—can be great for meditating beside. It symbolizes cleansing after a stressful day and will invite magical feminine energy.

• A firepit (or metal bucket you can safely have a small fire in) represents male fire energy. Use it for spells where you burn something. It will also provide warmth while you are outdoors in winter.

• Before you have an outdoor party, walk around the area three times clockwise. Each time, chant three times: "In this circle round, happiness and fun will abound!" You could also make and wear a daisy chain to ensure it'll be a fun event.

MAKE A WISH

To make your wishes come true, sing these words while you garden, or while looking at your potted plants:

Rose petals blooming red,

Around the garden, fate is lead.

Seeds of sun and flower gold,

By sacred spell my dreams unfold.

Magic takes root when planted,

And from the void a wish is granted.

PRACTICAL MAGIC **FAIRY GARDEN**

A fairy garden is a fun and whimsical magical space to create in your garden, and if you have children, they will love it too.

1 Create an area with pretty flowers and grasses, especially ones that attract butterflies and ladybugs.

Ferns are great, too, and are connected with the fairy folk.

2 Add a little birdhouse (perhaps decorated with a few feathers) to attract birds.

3 Decorate the space with windwheels, colored marbles, and homemade art, like painted stones or little statues. Be sure to avoid metal, especially iron and copper!

4 You could leave honey or sugar out for the fairies, if you need help finding a lost item, or want to ask them to keep your children or pets safe.

GARDEN MEDITATIONS

A garden can be a sanctuary and a wonderful place for meditation. Follow these tips to make your outside space a calming and meditative haven:

• Create a meditative labyrinth. If you have the space, you can make it big, with a low hedge or large stones, to walk through while chanting or meditating. Alternatively, you can keep it small, using pebblestones to just follow with your eyes. It can even be temporary and made with birdseed, just to look at for the day.

• To help create and maintain your garden as a lovely place to meditate, say the following each time you start gardening: "I seek quiet and calm, this place for my soul be a balm, I work to create a space to meditate."

• A calming, fragrant plant, like lavender or chamomile, may help you meditate. You can also dry it to make potpourri for meditating indoors during the winter!

ROSES

• Roses are easy to grow and are, of course, the prime love flower—pink for romantic love and red for passion. But don't forget that yellow roses will draw friendship and money to you, while white ones will bring pure energy.

• To safeguard your home, grow roses along your fence or up the walls of your house. Choose a variety with thorns to protect your home both literally (from intruders) and magically (from negativity and those with bad intentions).

• To strengthen the love between you and your partner, perhaps if you have been fighting recently or things have just gotten a bit dull, mix some rose petals (for love) with sugar (for the sweetness of a good relationship), nutmeg (for luck and keeping expectations realistic), and black pepper (to remove negativity). Sprinkle the mixture around your home, on the inside of doors and along windowsills.

Herbal heaven

Herbs can be used in myriad magical ways and can be grown outside or in pots on a windowsill.

MARJORAM

The Greek name for marjoram is *origanum* (and the cultivated garden version is oregano). The second part of the name, *ganos*, means joy, so this is a great herb to draw happiness to you. Use marjoram in salads and sauces served at a wake or memorial service: it will help those left behind to move on peacefully and remember the good times they had with the departed. You can also use it at any party to ensure a good time is had by all.

Dried marjoram mixed with peppermint and rosemary protects and attracts positive energy. Put some under the front doormat to protect your home from negative influences and people, and allow only joyous energy into the home. Alternatively, sprinkle the herbal mix over a treasured object to prevent it from being stolen or absorbing negative energy. (This is especially useful for tarot cards and other magical objects.)

CHAMOMILE

Chamomile is very useful, both as a medicinal herb and in magic, and it is a pretty flower that will adorn your garden. The yellow center of the flower symbolizes energy and the Sun God, while the white petals symbolize peace and the Moon Goddess.

Chamomile ensures that the souls of the dearly departed have an easier time getting used to being deceased, and enables a smooth transition to heaven. It is still planted on graves in Eastern Europe to this day and I tend to bury our small pets near my chamomile patch when they die.

If you need luck—be that for a card game or for a promotion (where you and a colleague have the same chance of getting the job)—wash your hands with chamomile soap or rub the flowers on your hands before the event.

PRACTICAL MAGIC **SOOTHING SCENT**

Chamomile tea can be a powerful potion to help you get rid of hexes and curses, negative energy in your home, or stress and bad feelings among co-workers.

1 Brew a cup of very strong chamomile tea.

2 Stir in a spoonful of honey counterclockwise.

3 Chant (in your head if you are at work and might be overheard!): "Stress and negativity, go away and let me be, curses here be none, all bad feelings be gone!"

4 Walk around your home or workplace, letting the steam of the tea waft everywhere.

PRACTICAL MAGIC **PURIFICATION SOAK**

Chamomile can be used to make a purifying bath and can help with anything from recovering after childbirth, and stressful events such as divorce, to ridding yourself of a bad relationship.

1 Place a good handful of dried chamomile in a muslin bag.

2 Hang the bag on the tap as you draw this ritual bath. (You can also sprinkle some nutmeg into the water for extra power.)

3 Get in and fully submerse yourself three times.

4 As you relax in the bath, say goodbye to the old you, any bad feelings you have about the events or person, and any pain you felt.

5 When you are ready, watch the water disappear down the drain, and with it, all stress and negativity.

PARSLEY

Do not be disheartened if your first attempt at growing parsley from seed or a cutting does not work out. One belief about parsley is that it must travel to hell and back seven times (or nine, if you ask some) before it will grow well for you and attain its magical strength and vigor. In fact, parsley has been associated with death in several cultures. Its strong scent was used to fragrance the room at wakes, and was said to help the soul move over and gain a good place in the underworld (or in heaven, depending on your religion).

If you have had lots of bad luck lately, just got out of a bad job or relationship, or are unsure how to figure out life, draw a warm bath and add a handful of freshly cut parsley. Stir it in counterclockwise as you say:

Bad luck, ill health, go away!

Fun and happiness, please stay!

As the Lord and Lady look after me,

The truth in everything I may see.

ROSEMARY

One of the few herbs that are green early in spring, a thriving rosemary plant is said to be proof of the Goddess pouring blessings on to a home. It's also a sign that the woman of the house is strong, for this is a witch's staple herb and at one time was thought to be indicative of a witch living in the house. Rosemary is an incredibly useful herb and can be used in a number of ways:

• A sprig of rosemary carried into a stressful situation, such as a job interview, gives courage.

• Dried rosemary sprinkled clockwise around a bed will help give restful sleep and chase away nightmares.

• I like to burn rosemary in my cauldron, together with crushed juniper berries and pine needles, to chase away colds.

THYME

The Victorians believed that thyme growing wild was a sign that fairies and elves were in the area. If you want to attract the little folk to your garden, plant thyme in a circle, and place something shiny in the middle—I favor a selection of brightly colored marbles. Thyme also has some other helpful qualities:

• To gain courage in a difficult situation—such as talking to a neighbor about noise, bringing a complaint at work, or for help in a legal battle—take a bath with thyme-infused oil or rub the oil onto your body.

• To attract fairies and draw their positive, playful energy into your life, place a sprig of thyme inside a house built from sugar cubes.

• To protect elderly family members or your children when they are at school, place a sprig of thyme in their pockets while chanting three times: "The protection of time I seek, for this person sweet and meek."

• Place a sprig of thyme under your pillow to protect from nightmares. It will bring restful sleep, and luck and courage to the next day.

DILL

The word dill comes from the old Norse word *dylla*, meaning to soothe or lull; dill fronds were once boiled with milk to soothe fussy children and anxious adults. These days, dill is a useful addition to any herb garden, bringing calm and luck to a variety of spells and charms.

Try making a braid using purple (for general luck), gold (for energy and luck coming quickly), or green (for general positivity) ribbon. Work dill fronds into the braid while chanting: "Change of luck, come to me! As I will it, so mote it be!" Hang the braid up or carry it with you in your pocket.

BASIL

Basil is the ultimate money herb and those needing to gain more income would be wise to grow this useful plant in their garden.

To attract money into the home, place five basil leaves and five copper coins under your front doormat. As you place down each coin and leaf, say:

Money, come to me,

Just as much as I need,

So I plant the seed.

Greedy I am not,

I don't need a lot.

Basil can be used in many other ways in and around the home:

• Prepare a dish using lots of basil. Spaghetti with pesto is especially good, as the yellow pasta symbolizes energy and inspiration. Eat it on a Thursday (the best day for money magic) before discussing your financial situation with your partner or family, or before asking for a pay rise.

• Sprinkle basil on windowsills and by the door before going out to keep the warmth inside the home, and to keep thieves out.

• Throw some basil leaves (dried is fine if you do not have fresh) into your open fire over the holidays to ward off negativity and prevent the festivities from costing you too much money.

• If you are reading tarot (or doing another divination) at the beginning of a new month or year to help figure out your path, place a basil leaf over each of your closed eyes as you consider the questions to ask.

LAVENDER

Lavender is my favorite herb, due to its beautiful purple color and sweet fragrance. You can make lavender sugar easily: layer dried lavender buds and sugar in a jar and let it sit in a dark place for about a month. Sift out the lavender buds and enjoy in delicately flavored cakes, whipped cream, custard, and tea. Try lavender honey, too: add a handful of lavender buds to a small jar of honey.

If you are facing a stressful situation, such as a meeting at work, a court case, or a party with a friend you have fallen out with, get a white handkerchief (white for peace and positive energy) and put five drops of lavender essential oil on it to symbolize each of the five points of the pentagram (earth, air, fire, water, spirit). Take the handkerchief out and sniff the lavender when things get stressful —this will keep you grounded and balanced.

If you are wondering about an old friend or family member you haven't heard from in a while, or had a fight with, draw a warm bath and add some sprigs of lavender, or a lavender-scented bath bomb. Relax and think positive thoughts about the person, asking the Messenger God, Mercury, to let you know how they are doing, or get them to contact you. Before you get out, submerge yourself fully three times and say:

[Name], I care for you,

My love for you still holds true.

Please let me know you are alright,

I only want positives, not a fight.

Magical pets

Witches love nature and tend to love animals, and keeping pets.
But pets are not just companions on a lonely evening—they can
also be companions in magic.

ANIMAL AFFINITY

Some pets have an affinity for magic, and from an early age want to actively help
with your spells or rituals. These pets have the potential to be what is called
a familiar: an animal that helps you do magic by channeling animal spirits to
assist you (the same way humans would ask fairies or deities to be present).
Familiars also lend their magical energy to a spell to make it more powerful.

The best way to "train" potential familiars is to simply let them be present
when you work a spell or do a ritual—even when (especially at the beginning)
they can be a little disruptive!

My cat Piggy, a black-and-white moggy, was a familiar. He started out wanting
to play with the tassels on my magical robe, but quickly learned to walk the
circle with me at the beginning of a ritual and would meow in each direction
as I called the elements. He was also very interested in tarot cards. At first,
I thought he just wanted to play with them but, by paying close
attention to what he did, I figured out that he was actually choosing
cards for me, especially when I did a reading for myself.

A simple spell with cats starts with petting them. When they
begin to purr, quietly say three times: "By the beauty of the
purr, good things will occur." If you have a specific issue or
outcome in mind, visualize it as you pet your feline friend.

PERFECT PETS

Many witches give preference to a black cat or dog when adopting. Because of their witchy associations, black cats can have difficulty finding a new home when they end up in a shelter. But it's not only dogs and cats that can become familiars. Any animal you deal with on a regular basis, or have a close connection with, can help you with your magic.

GOLDFISH: Kept in the north-facing part of your home, goldfish will help attract money and abundance from earth, the element of the north. Their color is significant: gold for money and prosperity, and orange for energy and justice. A pair of goldfish symbolizes that work and reward go together.

HORSE: Given reasonably free rein to carry you on its back, a horse may lead you to a wonderful forest glade ideal for meditation, or to a tree from which you can take a branch to make a wand with.

IGUANA: Iguanas, or other reptiles, can sit on your altar and be a visual focus for your magic.

A PAIR (OF ANY ANIMAL): Kept in the south-facing part of your home, two of any animal will assist in bringing and keeping love in your home, because south represents the fire element, and passion.

PRACTICAL MAGIC **FAMILIAR FRIENDSHIPS**

Of course, pets don't always get along, especially when you get a new one and the others are jealous! This spell can help with that.

1 Take a photo of your pets happy together. Alternatively, write all their names using blue ink on a white piece of paper.

2 Bind the paper or photo with yellow ribbon (to symbolize friendship).

3 Put this on your altar or in a nice sunny place to encourage friendship.

4 Add a couple of crystals into your pets' water bowls. For example, yellow carnelian (for friendship), rose quartz (to encourage love), or blue turquoise (to heal the relationship).

CHAPTER 2

Work Witchery

Whether you need help job hunting, setting up your
workspace, or dealing with stress at work, magic can help
you be your most productive and successful self!

Finding work

Work is such a crucial part of life. While you may not be actively looking for work or a new job every day, it is always a good idea to be open to new opportunities! Whether you need a new job or just want to keep your career options open, magic can help.

TIME FOR A CHANGE?

Death (XIII) is the 13th Major Arcana card in most traditional tarot decks. Contrary to what some people believe, this card isn't actually about death or bad luck, but about a major change in your life. By keeping this card in a prominent place, such as on your altar or with your work ID card or business clothes, you invite that change.

Another way to attract new work opportunities is to place a healthy green plant in a skull-shaped plant pot—look for one around Halloween! Or if you find a pretty animal skull during a walk in the woods, put it at the base of a plant. Watch the plant grow, and your opportunities grow with it.

PRACTICAL MAGIC **DREAM DIVINATIONS**

Allow your dreams to guide you on your career path.

1 Keep a pen and paper and a green candle (representing prosperity) on your nightstand.

2 Before going to bed, light the candle for a few minutes and look into the flame.

3 Ask the deities to guide you in your career search. You can call on whichever deities you feel close to but I recommend Vulcan (Roman god of work) or Epona and Lakshmi (goddesses of prosperity and happiness).

4 Safely extinguish the candle and go to sleep.

5 As soon as you wake up, write down and interpret any dreams you had. The deities will have given you hints in your dreams about what job or career path would suit you.

CARVE OUT A CAREER

You can carve candles with symbols that represent the job you are looking for, or the aspects of work that are important to you. For example, you could carve a house to represent that you want to work from home, two smiling stick figures if a friendly team is important to you, or a cat to signify that you want to work with animals. Once you have carved your candle, light it every day and chant the following words three times:

By the elements, water, earth, air, and fire,

Bring to me the job I desire.

I will have happiness, wealth, and ways to grow,

This is my will, now make it so!

Another good job-finding spell is to carve the word "work" into an apple, plus any requirements, such as your desired salary or working hours. Then bury the apple near a healthy, sturdy tree. As the apple gets absorbed by Mother Earth, it will send out positive job energy for you. Alternatively, you could bury the apple in a significant place, such as near a factory you'd love to work in, or in the direction of where you'd like to find work.

CANDLE COLOR

While a green candle will bring prosperity, you could choose a color that corresponds to your desired career field.

BLUE:
A job in health care.

BROWN:
Working outside.

GOLD:
A role in finance.

FIND YOUR DREAM JOB

Are you eyeing another job but are not sure whether you should leave your current one? Or perhaps you have been lucky enough to be offered two jobs. With a blue pen (blue is associated with wisdom), write down five positive and three negative things about each job. Sleep with the list under your pillow and you may dream about the correct position, or wake up with certainty that one is definitely not for you.

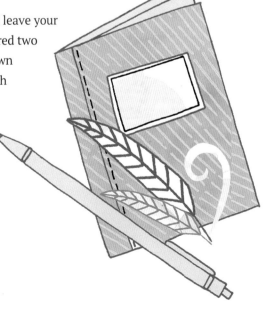

Setting up your workspace

There are many things you cannot control about your workspace, especially if you work in a factory or office cubicle. But no matter your profession or work setup, you can make your area more magical with some easy tweaks.

WHAT TO WEAR

Consider the clothes you wear to work. Or your underwear, if there is a uniform policy! The color is important, of course (see box below). Jewelry can also bring magic to your work day. Try the simple tips below and see the box on the next page.

• Wear earrings if you want to improve your listening skills or get someone to listen to you.

• An anklet will ground you in reality.

• A bracelet worn on the left arm will help you to listen to your emotions and take the emotions of others into account. A bracelet on the right arm will help you to be more decisive and take action.

WORK WARDROBE

Wear clothes in colors that reflect your intention for the day.

YELLOW: To make friends at work.

WHITE: For peace.

BLACK: To absorb negativity from customers or a picky boss.

RED: To be noticed more by your boss, or by customers on the sales floor.

TYPES OF JEWELRY

Embrace the magical properties of your jewelry collection.

GOLD: Attracts financial and general business success.

SILVER: Hones your intuition, helping you to find good opportunities.

PLATINUM: Helps you to be a strong leader.

AMBER: Diffuses tension in the office.

BLACK OBSIDIAN: Absorbs negativity.

JADE AND EMERALD: Attract money to you.

YOUR DESK

If your job is deskbound, you have a lot of options when it comes to decorating your working environment in a witchy way!

Consider animal objects as decoration to gain the assistance of the animal spirits. For example:

• A photo of your dog on your desk will increase the loyalty of those working for you.

• A pendant of a bear will keep you strong in the face of adversity.

• A drawing of an eagle on your wall will allow you to see the bigger picture.

• A white feather will bring peace and contentment to the office.

CRYSTAL COMPANIONS

You can keep crystals anywhere on your desk. If they turn pale and lose their color, recharge them by washing them under water then burying them in salt for a few days. Leave them out in the sunlight and moonlight before using them again.

CLEAR QUARTZ: To gain more energy and attract positive attention.

TIGER'S EYE: For general business success.

HEMATITE: To feel more grounded and stay on task.

CITRINE: To make customers or co-workers be more friendly toward you.

AMETHYST: To absorb excess radiation and keep the computer running well (if you work on a computer or with other electronics).

PRACTICAL MAGIC **DESK PLANT**

Keep a leafy green plant on your desk. It will attract money and success at work, and will also help to keep you calm.

1 Choose a low-maintenance plant that is suitable for the conditions in your workplace and place it on your desk.

2 Strengthen its simple magic by adding a few copper coins to the soil of the plant to increase your financial success.

3 Add some crystals to decorate the pot (see box, page 47).

4 Sit back and watch your success at work grow, just like your plant!

DON'T FORGET OFFICE SUPPLIES!

I love having sticky notes in many different colors. They are versatile and can be used around an office in many ways. It is also useful to keep different colored pens to hand, particularly in colors that correspond with your magical and business aims.

• I like to put a sticky note up without anything written on it, just to bring the magical significance of the color to me.

• Write a quick chant, or draw a rune that symbolizes peace or success, on a sticky note, and stick it behind your computer or under your desk where no one can see.

• To find balance, maybe between what your boss and your client wants, or to improve your work-life balance, use four colored sticky notes to symbolize the four elements being balanced—blue for water, green for earth, white or yellow for air, and red for fire.

• Unless you have to use a specific color—perhaps to sign legal documents—use pens in different colors (that are tailored to your aims) to write your notes.

• If you are dealing with a lot of negativity from those you work with, make a pentagram on your desk out of office supplies to symbolize the four elements and spirit. This will help your co-workers to balance their emotions and demands.

CLEAR THE AIR

Harness the power of scent and flavor in your working space to sweeten the air—both literally and magically!

• While you can't burn incense at your desk (unless you work from home), you can make yourself a nice cup of herbal tea (see box below). Alternatively, use essential oils in a diffuser, or a drop on your office chair, for a similar result.

• Sprinkle rose water around discreetly. It cleanses the space of negativity and brings positive energy—and most people, if they smell it, will just think that someone has got a bouquet of flowers!

• Sweeten up picky customers, stressed co-workers, or a demanding boss with a bowl of white peppermint candy or licorice to clear the air and reduce negativity. When a negative person takes a piece, chant the following in your head: "I deserve respect, my work deserves respect, you will respect my space and job!"

HERBAL HELP

PEPPERMINT: If there is negativity and strife in the office, walk around with a steaming cup of peppermint tea to clear the air.

CHAMOMILE: If it's a stressful week, brew chamomile tea.

ORANGE PEKOE: To get justice in a work dispute, drink broken orange pekoe tea.

BAY LEAF: To get the project you want, add a bay leaf to your tea of choice.

Magical productivity and success

Working life can have its ups and downs, but there are lots of things you can do to help yourself thrive at work!

MANIFEST YOUR SUCCESS

If you need extra success at work, or for a good thing to happen in your job, make a figure of yourself out of yellow clay (yellow being the color of success). Leave the figure out in the moonlight to be blessed with the intuition of the Moon Goddess who will show the way in the darkness. Also leave it in direct sunlight, to be blessed with the confidence and energy of the Sun God. If money is the main aim, sit the figure on two copper coins (one for each foot) and put a coin on its head as well, so that money is above and below it. This symbolizes you being surrounded with all the money you need.

FINANCE

Thursday is a fortuitous day for finance, as is the color green. Deal with anything money-related (such as paying bills, asking for a raise, or for a loan from the bank) on a Thursday, if you can. Similarly, place lots of green around your place of work:

- Place a round-leafed green (and healthy!) plant by the front of your store.

- Keep the documents relating to your start-up business in a green folder.

- Paint the front door of your business premises green.

- Hang a green ribbon on the door to your office.

To combine the financial power of Thursday with the color green, etch the amount of money you need onto a green candle, and light it for a few minutes on a Thursday during a waxing moon. As the moon increases in the sky, so will your finances. To ensure continuing financial stability and success, repeat every Thursday thereafter.

PRACTICAL MAGIC **REQUEST A PAY RISE**

Be realistic! Only ask for what you need or what you think your department can afford. Remember, magic only increases probability, it doesn't make anything certain. If you ask for a realistic, market-appropriate raise, you have a good chance of getting it—if you ask for an extra million dollars or pounds per month, even the most powerful witch is unlikely to get that!

1 Etch a currency symbol into a beeswax candle (beeswax represents luxury and wealth).

2 Set the candle on a white plate (for pure energy) to increase the magical power of the spell.

3 Light the candle once a week, preferably on a Sunday (for business success—see page 119), and again on the days you ask for the raise and expect to receive a response.

4 Repeat step 3 until you get the raise.

5 For extra power, as you get ready for work each morning, visualize your boss coming to you and offering you the raise. This works especially well on a waxing moon.

KNOTS AND RIBBONS

To attract business success or do well in professional exams, knot spells work well. Try one of these three spells using ribbons.

Nine knots

There is a standard chant for ribbon magic, which can be used for almost any kind of intent or goal.

1 Hold a piece of ribbon or cord in your hands and think about what you want to achieve, or stop from happening.

2 Make nine knots in the cord, as you chant the words below.

By the knot of one, the spell's begun,

By the knot of two, it becomes true,

By the knot of three, so mote it be,

By the knot of four, magic energy I store,

By the knot of five, it comes alive,

By the knot of six, the energies fix,

By the knot of seven, sun and moon in heaven,

By the knot of eight, I call the powers of fate,

By the knot of nine, this spell is mine.

3 Leave the knotted cord on your altar or in a safe place at work where it will not be disturbed.

4 When the spell has worked its magic and you have achieved your goal, unmake the knots and bury the cord under a tree.

Making money

Use this spell to become more prosperous and retain money for your family or your business, rather than spending it unwisely. Use a copper coin if you want more energy and resources coming to you, or a silver coin if you want to make it easier to save or spend less.

1 Tie a wide, green ribbon around a coin so it is completely hidden in the ribbon.

2 Make a knot on one side of the ribbon package and say: "I make this knot, spend I will not."

3 Then make a knot on the other side and say: "Money comes to me, as I will it, so mote it be!"

Lunar assistance

For this knot spell you will need three colored ribbons: blue for wisdom, yellow for inspiration, and silver for the protection of the Moon Goddess.

1 Braid the three ribbons together.

2 As you braid, think about your business or professional exams going well. Visualize being calm and feeling content with how you did after.

3 Make a knot in the newly made braid for each exam or each step toward your work goal.

4 Put the ribbon on your altar or in a drawer in your desk at work. Unmake the knots on the day you will receive the results of your project or exam.

SWEET (AND SAVORY) SUCCESS

Raid your store cupboard for some magical ingredients.

ALMONDS: To attract business success, carry five almonds, preferably still in their shell, on the left side of your body, such as in a pants pocket.

HONEY: The golden color and sweetness of honey symbolize business success, money, and the sweetness of doing well. Simply eat a little honey each day, or try the honey jar spell (see page 55).

SPICES: To bring positive attention to yourself at work, sprinkle some cinnamon on your tools, work papers, or around your work computer. Then, rub the cinnamon away with a piece of ginger—freshly cut is best, but dried or candied should work too. This will bring positive energy and the strength of the Sun God to your work.

HERBS: Add herbs to your food, and stir in clockwise to gain the positive energy from them. Fresh parsley represents both physical and symbolic fertility, and can help you to come up with better ideas, or help your job to become more interesting. Basil brings financial and business success, and bay leaves encourage general success or being the best at something. If you don't like eating these herbs, plant some in your garden, keep a pot in your office, or keep them with your job ID card or business papers to promote creative ideas at work.

See pages 19–30 and pages 34–39 in Chapter 1 to read about other magical ingredients!

PRACTICAL MAGIC **MAKE A HONEY JAR**

Have a go at this honey jar spell to help you achieve your ambitions and do well at work.

1 In a small jar, add a few coins to symbolize money and some salt to represent hard work.

2 Collect some symbols of what you are trying to achieve. For example, a key for owning your own store, a blue marble to symbolize traveling around the world with your job, or a few hairs from your dog to attract a job where you can work from home and have time to walk him or her!

3 Pop the items in the jar and add honey to cover them.

4 Seal the jar and keep it somewhere safe until you gain the success you are looking for.

MAGICAL TIPS FOR BUSINESS SUCCESS

Do you have your own business and want to magically help its success?

• Keep a statue or picture of the god Hermes in your office or store. If this is not possible, due to customers that may disapprove, you can be more covert—draw little wings (a symbol of this Greek god) on your shoes or behind your ears.

• Include yellow or gold in your business logo. A round logo represents dynamic success and adaptability while a square shape symbolizes steadiness and reliability.

• Money attracts money, so always keep some money wherever you work. For example, keep a few coins in your workshop under your tools, in your car if you drive from client to client, or in the till even when your store is closed.

• Have something sweet nearby—either a candy as you work or a little sugar sprinkled on your doorstep—to symbolize the sweetness of a job well done and a successful business.

• Do you often have to go around your whole office, maybe to distribute mail, or are you responsible for cleaning your workspace? If yes, do so clockwise if you want to increase cooperation, or counterclockwise to decrease stress and negativity.

APPLE DIVINATION

To divine the future success of your business, peel an apple slowly while thinking about a particular question or issue. Choose the color of apple that best suits your question: green if the issue is to do with money, yellow if it involves co-workers or general business success, and red if it relates to a passion project or long-term career goals. Throw the peel over your right shoulder and interpret how it falls:

• If the peel falls like a perfect circle on the ground, then that could symbolize prosperity (the circle representing a coin).

• If the peel falls in a twisted shape like an ampersand (&) sign, it means you need help with your business.

• The peel may fall close to an object, such as a bookshelf, meaning you need to read and learn more, or near a photo of a person, symbolizing that they can help.

• If the peel falls apart as you throw it, this may mean that your plan is destined to fail.

PRACTICAL MAGIC **ELEMENTS MEDITATION**

Don't neglect one part of your business in favor of the other parts, because this would eventually lead to failure. The quick meditation below will make sure you have thought of everything.

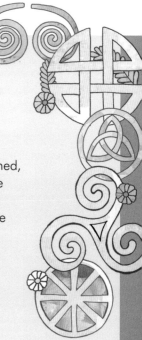

1 Stand with your feet hip-width apart in the middle of your office or workplace.

2 Breathe in and out deeply several times to still your mind.

3 Visualize the element of earth to the north of you, air to the east of you, fire to the south, and water to the west. Is one of them stronger? If fire seems warmer or bigger, perhaps you are too passionate and not thinking logically about your business; or if earth seems to encroach on air and water, perhaps you are too traditional and conservative in your business dealings.

4 When you have finished, feel the Sun God above you and the Earth Goddess below you give you their blessings for a successful business.

Combatting work stress

Working life can be stressful. Try to find some time for yourself during the work day. Go for a walk and deliberately walk slowly, even if it is just from your desk to the bathroom.

SLOW IT DOWN

If you are getting overwhelmed working on a project or studying for an exam, light a yellow candle by your desk and spend a few moments looking into it while recalling information you have read. Then write this chant at the top of your work papers:

Lord and Lady, make me clear of sight,

Come forth to fill my mind with wisdom bright,

To keep my mind alert and clear,

I know I have nothing to fear,

With this [learning/working] I ask, may my senses be keen,

I write these words to come into being.

At the end of the working day, have a bath, and take your time in it! Adding some geranium or peppermint oil to the water will help remove negative thinking and make you feel more positive and motivated to face challenges. As the water drains from the bathtub, visualize your stress and negative energy draining away, leaving you clean in body and spirit to start afresh.

You could also try adding a few drops of lavender essential oil to your clothing to calm you before you start the next working day.

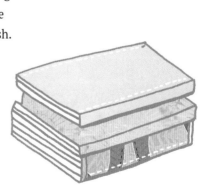

PRACTICAL MAGIC
FIVE-MINUTE STRESS BUSTER

This is a great visualization to do when you are having a hard day at the office, or when customers are running you ragged! It is best done while making a cup of calming tea, such as peppermint or chamomile, but can be done with a bowl of soup for lunch or even with a cup of water and a spoon.

1 Stand with both your feet solidly on the ground, about hip-width apart. Feel yourself fully connected to the earth, which is providing you with strength and calming love.

2 With your hot drink (or soup) in front of you, stir it counterclockwise, imagining all the negativity and stress flowing out of you. Visualize it flowing out of your head and body, down your arm and into your hand, then the spoon, and then into the cup.

3 Stop stirring and smell the brew. Realize that even though there is negativity in there, it is still a yummy drink, just as while there may be stress and negativity in your life, you still have many blessings.

4 Add honey or sugar, if appropriate. When you feel ready, start stirring again, but clockwise this time. Imagine happiness and positive energy building up in the cup, traveling up through the spoon and into your hand, then up your arm and through your whole body.

5 Drink your witch's brew and be happy and calm!

MANAGE OFFICE CONFLICT

Are you having a bad time at work? Do your colleagues sometimes put you down, or are you suffering from impostor syndrome? Perhaps you want to go for a promotion, but your colleagues say you can't do it, or maybe you have failed to get a raise three times and are feeling unsure about asking again.

Whatever the source of your worry may be, go to the bathroom and look at yourself in the mirror, or just use a compact mirror if you have one. Smile at yourself and nod as if acknowledging the person in the mirror as a person to be respected. Then say the below words three times—out loud if you can, or in your head if you think someone will overhear:

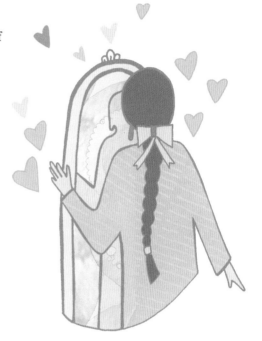

I am an expert in my field,

Success I will yield!

Negativity will harm me none,

My will be done!

Good things will come to be,

As I will it, so mote it be!

If you need justice in a work dispute, make a traditional Christmas pomander. Stick negativity-busting cloves into an orange or mandarin (as orange is the color of justice) while thinking about the issue and what you can do to make it better. Leave it at work until the issue is resolved, then eat the fruit if it is still good, or leave it out for the wildlife if not. While the dispute is still going on, keep a piece of oak wood on your desk to remind you to stay strong.

Another way to ward off any bad energy from nasty co-workers is to add some drops of clove oil to your clothing, or carry whole cloves in your pocket.

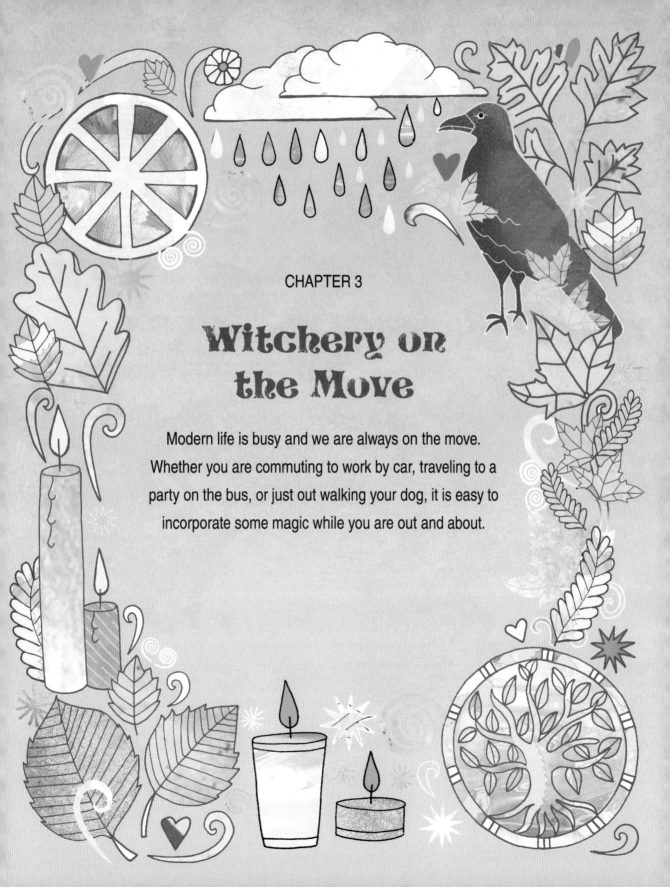

CHAPTER 3

Witchery on the Move

Modern life is busy and we are always on the move.
Whether you are commuting to work by car, traveling to a
party on the bus, or just out walking your dog, it is easy to
incorporate some magic while you are out and about.

Traveling by car

More and more of us travel by car, and that can be very stressful! If driving stresses you out, there are many ways you can keep yourself calm and magically occupied when you're on the road.

DRIVING WHATEVER THE WEATHER

Weather conditions can have a big impact on our driving experience and resulting stress levels. If it is raining, imagine the rainwater is cleaning your car, and your mind, by washing away all negativity and stress. If the sun is in your eyes, making it difficult to see, slow down and visualize the sun's rays as the Sun God's gift of warmth, light, and protection.

PRACTICAL MAGIC **PARKING CHARM**

When you have arrived at your destination, call on the fairies if you need a little help finding a place to park.

1 Keep a piece of chocolate, a sugar packet, or another sweet treat in your car.

2 As you are looking for a parking spot, chant: "Parking fairy, I am in a bind, but a parking space I will find!"

3 Once you have parked, drop the sweet treat by the curb, giving thanks to the parking fairy.

SHARING THE ROAD

There is only so much we can do, magically or otherwise, about bad drivers! But if someone cuts you off or seems to be showing road rage toward you, remember the Threefold Law of Wicca: "Anything you do reflects three times onto you." This is basically our version of karma. Look into your rearview or side mirrors and imagine that the aggression and negativity of the other driver is being reflected back onto them.

ENCHANT YOUR CAR

Add a magical touch to the interior and exterior of your car with these simple tips.

CONSIDER THE COLOR: A gray car can calm you, a black one absorbs negativity, while a white car brings positive energy. A pale blue car can help with inspiration, and a red one will help to bring passion into your life.

ADD A DECORATIVE DECAL (STICKER): Adding a pentagram decal to your bumper will provide general protection, or a triple moon (waxing, full, and waning moon) decal will bring the blessing of the Goddess.

USE TURQUOISE FOR PROTECTION: Keep a piece of turquoise in your glove box to help prevent accidents. Check on it if you have a near collision because you may need a new one—it is said that the turquoise will break instead of the car or person driving.

MAKE AN AIR FRESHENER: Fill a round, gold-colored tea infuser with rosemary, cloves, and lavender, then hang it on your rearview mirror. The rosemary and cloves will ward off negativity and prevent accidents, the lavender will calm you, and the gold color of the infuser symbolizes the protection and self-confidence of the Sun God.

PERSONALIZE YOUR CAR KEY CHAIN: Add a symbol of your favorite god or goddess to your key chain—a small piece of jade, for example, which is associated with the hunter goddess Diana. Or add a figure of an animal you feel drawn to. You could choose a black cat to increase your magical intuition and protection, a bear to keep you strong, or a salmon for quick reactions while driving.

Traveling by public transport

Traveling by bus, train, or subway can be less stressful than traveling by car or being stuck in traffic, and it gives you time to study witchy books like this one or practice meditation. However, overcrowded trains and delayed buses can bring their own challenges.

PASSENGER PROTECTION

Magically protecting your clothing and belongings can help you to feel safe and calm while traveling on public transport.

• Anoint your shoes, scarf, jacket, water bottle, or umbrella (or any other item you use while on the go) with a single drop of a protection oil such as cedar, sandalwood, or rosemary. If you don't want to put oil directly onto your belongings, add the oil to a small piece of black cloth (to absorb negative energy) and tuck the cloth into your shoes or pocket.

• Speak a blessing (see below) over your items for extra protection.

• You could also attach nettle leaves to your clothes and visualize them keeping bad people and negative energy away. But be very careful not to touch the stinging side of the leaves.

May steps I take and [item] I wear,

Blessed be by water, earth, fire, and air,

Whether aimed west, north, south, or east,

I am safely armored and fully free.

PRACTICAL MAGIC
CALMING BUBBLE OF PROTECTION

Whether you are sitting at a bus stop or on the subway, you can create a protective shield with this easy incantation.

1 Imagine roots reaching down from where you are sitting. Visualize these roots digging deep down into the earth.

2 Visualize a light coming from above you—from the sun if you can see it.

3 Imagine pulling both energies (from above and below you) into your body and building a shield around you in protective colors, such as white for pure energy, blue for health, yellow to keep people friendly, or purple for occult protection.

4 Allow the shield to circle around you and then, when you feel ready, end with the incantation: "This protective shield shall stay with me in my day, and so shall it be."

MAGIC IN YOUR MOVEMENTS

Buses, trains, and their stations can be utilized for magic in a number of different ways.

• Find a public transport route that goes clockwise around your local area. You can use the journey to "charge" a magical tool, such as your wand or a gemstone, to use in a spell later. Or travel counterclockwise around the area to help you remove any negative energy. There is no need to attract attention to what you are doing. Simply hold your chosen object in your hands and chant any spells in your head.

• You can use the urban landscape for divination. Lots of bus stops and tunnels are covered in graffiti, and you can view these tags as modern-day magical sigils. Interpret their typography and color, perhaps to help determine how your day will go, how to get a promotion, or what to do at the weekend.

• Pick up a free newspaper at the train station or look at the next billboard you go past. The first letter of the headline could provide a hint for the future.

Waiting around

Witches get just as bored as anyone else while waiting around for their drink in the coffee shop line, in the doctor's waiting room, or any other place we have to queue. But this time can be used productively!

MEDITATIVE MOMENTS

Meditations, visualizations, and divination are great ways to spend your time while you are sitting or standing around.

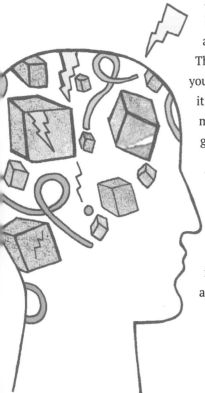

• Practice a bit of divination by scrolling quickly through one of your social media platforms while thinking of a question or issue. For your answer, interpret where the scroll stops. Is it a cute cat meme? Then maybe the issue isn't as big as you thought it was. Is it a photo of a family member? Then take this as a sign to ask your family for help! Or perhaps it is a workout video? If so, you might need to work harder to get the issue solved.

• To use music for divination, quickly turn on a radio, use shuffle on your playlist, or skip to a random part of a favorite song. What you immediately hear will provide an important message for you.

• To get in touch with ancestors, local spirits, or your patron deity, get into a trance-like state through repetitive movement. This could be crocheting, twirling your thumbs, or listening to trance music. Take note of what snaps you out of your trance for a hint of what the future brings.

• Carry your tarot cards with you (or just a standard deck of playing cards) and train yourself to get better at card reading. Think of a question that you know you will find the answer to shortly, such as, "Will a man or a woman sit next to me?" or "What will the weather be like when I arrive?" Then, draw a card to get the answer. If you are already skilled with tarot, think of an actual issue or more difficult question while you shuffle, then draw the card.

PRACTICAL MAGIC **POSITIVE THOUGHTS**

Ground yourself with a meditation to remove the stress and anxiety of waiting.

1 Stand solidly with your feet hip-width apart and take nine deep breaths in and out, filling your lungs completely.

2 With each breath in, imagine the white light of pure, positive energy entering your body through your nose, filling your lungs, and from there, moving into the rest of your body.

3 As you exhale through your mouth, imagine your daily stress, problems, and negative energy, thoughts, and emotions as black smoke leaving your body, being dispersed into the world where the spirits can recycle it into positive energy.

4 Take nine more deep breaths in and out, but this time, imagine all the pure energy staying within you, filling you from your core.

PRACTICAL MAGIC **RAISE THE ENERGY**

Use this energy exercise to make sure you get noticed by those you are waiting for, or to avoid falling asleep while queuing.

1 Stand comfortably. Imagine a circle around you on the ground, glowing with energy.

2 Imagine it starting to rise around you and slowly rotate in a clockwise circle.

3 Imagine the cone of energy encasing you, and when it does, close your eyes and feel the warmth of the cone around you, its light and energy entering you.

4 When you have all the energy you need, feel the cone slowly sink into the ground, taking any excess energy with it.

5 Open your eyes, full of energy and ready to continue your day.

Traveling on foot

Whether you are walking to work or school, to meet a friend, or just for the exercise and fresh air, pay attention to the nature around you.

WALK WITH NATURE

When you find something green sprouting in an unlikely place, stop and take some time to appreciate it. It doesn't matter if it's just a weed in a crack in the sidewalk, some moss by a drain, a potted plant in a window, or some grass on a lawn or public park—gain strength from how the plants persevere. As you walk, try this quick chant to help you gain balance and invite magic into your life:

May the sun high in the air,

Give me the strength to dare.

May the oceans of my soul,

Be healed and make me whole.

When you come to a crossroads, stay a few minutes if you have time. Close your eyes and just let your mind drift, thinking about any changes in your life and what to do about them.

After a while, you will feel drawn to open your eyes. Look around you, and take hints from your surroundings about what you should do next:

• The shapes of the clouds overhead might show you where you should go or what job you should take, for example.

• Be guided by the color of a car or some flowers you see nearby, such as blue for healing or red for putting more passion into your relationship.

• Maybe you'll see a colony of busy ants telling you to work harder to get the money you need for your goals.

WALKING THE DOG

Animals can be familiars (see page 40) and help you in fortune-telling and magic. An easy way to divine the future is to let your dog lead you where it wants to when out on a walk, or watch your cat as it wanders around the yard. Pick up hints from how your pets behave and what they sniff!

• Are they interested in yellow flowers or leaves? This signals that you should pay more attention to your friendships, yellow being the color of friendship.

• Are they looking at a red "stop" sign? This might literally mean stop, or may point toward love, due to its red color.

• Are they walking in circles? This could be a sign to circle back on previous issues or answers you have received.

Nature as an oracle

In witchcraft, all plants and animals are sacred because they are part of Mother Nature. Many herbs and plants turn up in mythological tales too. The plants and birds you come across while out in nature can provide some general insight into your life, or help with a specific issue you are facing.

HOW TO HEAR NATURE'S MESSAGES

There are several ways you can use nature as your oracle:

• Go out for a walk and see how many different plants, flowers, trees, and birds (listed on pages 71–77) you can find. Touch each plant or tree as you find it and watch the birds. If you feel positive about, or "magically drawn" to a particular one, it will be trying to tell you something!

• For a hint of what is to come in your life, go to a park or other place of nature that you have never been to before. Take note of the first plant you come across and consider what message it might hold for you. You could also do the same thing if you are on your way to meet a new friend or to a new job.

• Listen to your intuition. If a plant or animal ever "calls to you" while you are going about your day, always stop and pay attention to what it is trying to tell you.

EARTH ELEMENT

To ensure a safe journey, especially when traveling far away, carry a little soil with you from home if you can.

Take it from a place that means a lot to you, be that your garden, a favorite houseplant, or the local park where you like to read.

Add the soil to your luggage with a wish to return home safe, and request the protection of the Earth Goddess on your journey. Return the soil to its original place when you get back.

PLANTS AND FLOWERS

Plants have distinct meanings and are often used in alternative medicine and magic. They are associated with particular elements and deities based on their color, where they grow, what they look like, or their role in mythological stories.

BLUEBELL: This flower is a symbol of loyalty, gratitude, and everlasting love. Being drawn to bluebells could mean that someone you are not sure about truly loves you, or that someone will finally give you the thanks you deserve. Don't pick bluebells—fairies are said to be jealous of those that do, and will destroy the love others hold for you!

BUTTERCUP: This yellow flower brings friends closer together and reminds those that have grown apart of the wonder of friendships. If buttercups appeal to you, get in touch with old friends you haven't seen for a while, or make an effort to strengthen new friendships, perhaps by using buttercup petals as a table decoration when having new friends over.

COWSLIP: This flower symbolizes purity and truthfulness. If you feel drawn to it, this could be a warning not to cut corners or tell that little white lie you have been considering, but to stay moral and ethical in your dealings. Add cowslip flowers to a salad to purify yourself before a ritual or after completing an unpleasant task.

DAFFODIL: Symbolizing hope and renewal as well as rebirth, daffodils are the ultimate spring flower. They remind us that a new season has arrived. This is a good time to effect a major change in your life, do a big clean out of your home, or start a difficult relationship afresh.

DAISY: If you feel drawn to the daisy, you should take things less seriously, and bring more joy into your life! Go out and have some fun, spend a little money on a frivolous purchase, or play a harmless practical joke on someone. Make and wear a daisy chain at a picnic or party to ensure it'll be a fun event!

NETTLE: This plant warns of negative people or influences that will come your way, such as a new co-worker you should avoid or an impending visit from a friend who has negative feelings. If the nettle plant stands out to you, be watchful and protect yourself. Tie some nettle flowers to a mirror to reflect any negativity or curses back to the sender.

PRIMROSE: A warning that there is danger or uncomfortable situations ahead, the primrose also gives hope that you can get through it as long as you have confidence in yourself and your abilities. Life will be better for you when the situation has passed. Wear a purple primrose in your buttonhole or jacket pocket to protect from curses and negative magic.

VIOLET: This plant, and other purple flowers such as thistles, urges you to keep an open mind. Being drawn to it may mean that you should look at a problem from another angle, or if you had a recent disagreement with somebody, that you should consider their point of view. Meditate with a purple flower on your crown chakra to be shown a new path.

TREES

Trees are full of wisdom and understanding, some living for thousands of years.

APPLE: These trees symbolize immortality and also herald visits from the dead. If you feel drawn to apple trees, it may be because someone from the afterlife (perhaps an ancestor or recently departed friend) is trying to contact you.

CHERRY: Cherry blossom signifies fun and love to come, but later on, when the tree fruits. Stay lighthearted about your quest for love and plan some activities that bring you joy over the next few months. Who knows, you may find love while you are having fun! Cherries signal more passion is on its way, or that more passion is needed to bring success to a project.

CHESTNUT: This tree promises abundance and luxuries to come. If you are drawn to a chestnut tree and you are having financial difficulties, or going through a hard time at work, do not worry—things will resolve themselves. Carry a single chestnut tree leaf in your wallet or place it under your doormat to draw money to you.

HAWTHORN: The hawthorn blesses and protects those who have an affinity to it, especially children, young couples, and pregnant women. If you feel fearful or unsure about a venture and this tree stands out to you, do not be afraid! Everything will work out well.

MAGNOLIA: Magnolia is a love bush. If a purple-flowering magnolia appeals to you, this signifies new opportunities for finding a soulmate, while the pink-flowering magnolia heralds the chance to make a friendship or working relationship into something more loving. To keep a partner faithful, place some magnolia under the bed.

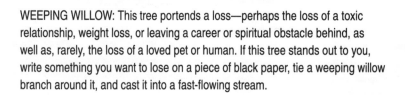

OAK: This tree is the traditional meeting place for outdoor rituals due to its strength and steadfastness. An oak tree tells you to believe in yourself, have confidence in your abilities, and give yourself credit! It serves as a reminder that "from small acorns, mighty oaks do grow," so start off small and let your plans or relationship grow naturally. To help wishes come true, imagine planting an acorn and it growing into a strong oak tree under your care.

WEEPING WILLOW: This tree portends a loss—perhaps the loss of a toxic relationship, weight loss, or leaving a career or spiritual obstacle behind, as well as, rarely, the loss of a loved pet or human. If this tree stands out to you, write something you want to lose on a piece of black paper, tie a weeping willow branch around it, and cast it into a fast-flowing stream.

WITCH HAZEL: Branches from witch hazel trees are used in dowsing. If you feel drawn to this tree, you should find out more about a plan, new job, or friend before pursuing it, and be cautious until you find out everything there is to know. If you have lost something, throw a witch hazel branch into the air and it will land pointing in the direction of the lost item.

BIRDS

Birds are especially important when divining, because they are a symbol of air and inspiration. They play a central part in many creation myths and are messengers for the gods to the humans and the underworld.

BLACKBIRD: This bird is a sign of spirituality bringing good luck, so if it stands out to you, take some time to read a religious book or look into divination courses. Finding a blackbird nest near your home is a signal of good fortune. If you find an abandoned nest, take it into your home to have good luck all year round—and play the lottery! Place a blackbird feather in someone's clothes to get them to open up to you and tell you what is bothering them.

BLUE TIT: These colorful birds are the guardian birds of young women. If you know any teenage girls, and you find yourself drawn to this bird, this is a sign she may need you. If you are a young woman yourself, listen to the bird's chirping because it may have a message for you. The blue tit's blue plumage serves as a reminder to take care of your health, so have a healthy dinner, and if you have not been feeling well, make an appointment with your doctor!

COLLARED DOVE: This bird symbolizes love and peace, but its collar also reminds us that sometimes we must restrain ourselves to gain this. If you see a collared dove, you may need to tone down your outspokenness, or work harder toward compromise to gain peace with your family or strengthen the love between you and your partner. If you are single and looking for love, try to hear a dove coo on a Friday to help love find its way to you.

CROW: Crows are associated with death and war. If you see a single crow, it heralds a fight to come; if you see a murder (group) of crows, someone is actively working against you so guard yourself. Try not to cause a murder of crows to take flight, as this is said to stir up trouble. To guard against fights in your home, wrap a crow's feather in blue cloth (for healing and wisdom), and tie it with white string (for peace).

JAY: These birds chatter, and a jay crossing your path from left to right means someone is talking behind your back; one crossing from right to left means you should be careful what you say about others. If you want help with poor eyesight, or to gain the "second sight," dip a jay feather in holy water and brush it lightly onto your closed eyes.

LONG-TAILED TIT: These birds are almost always found in groups and have been called "avian sheep"—a reminder that we don't always need to lead, but also should not be alone. Breeding pairs of long-tailed tits receive help from others that have no eggs that season. Take this as a sign that if you have a friend or family member who is alone or needs help with their children or house, now would be the time to go and help them.

MAGPIE: Associated with unhappiness and bad luck (as per the rhyme "One for Sorrow"), if this bird stands out to you, especially if flying in a circle, be careful with your possessions. Don't be fooled by something or someone with a "shiny" exterior that may bring you short-term happiness—look closer at your life to find long-lasting joy and deep contentment. To avoid bad luck when seeing a magpie, salute it, turn in a circle, and touch something wooden.

MALLARD: Ducks are sacred to the Sun God. Being drawn to them means you have his blessing in your endeavor, and you should stop doubting yourself. Their gracefulness in the female element of water also portends a visit or relationship with a sensitive man, so be open to a new man coming into your life. To have the Sun God bless your home, hang a mallard feather, quill up, where the morning sun can shine on it.

PIGEON: Seeing a pigeon to the left of a tree signals a bad day to come or that there is a fault in your plan. If you see one to the right of a tree, this is a sign you will have a good day and are on a prosperous path. A pigeon pecking on your window portends health issues, so take some extra vitamin C and be careful when out and about. Sleeping on pigeon feathers keeps illness at bay, so gather a few and slip them into your pillowcase, but make sure you sterilize them first!

ROBIN: This bird will bring fun and light-hearted love your way. If one attracts your attention, take this as a sign that you should lighten up and make some time for social activities in your life. With regard to relationships, it means you will find love soon, but it won't be a serious relationship, at least for a while. Make a wish when seeing the first robin in spring. If you can finish your wish before the bird flies away, it will come true by next spring.

SEAGULL: The seagull is a messenger between us and the deities. Being drawn to one indicates you should pay attention to your spiritual side, as there is a message for you. Do a meditation to talk to your favorite goddess, or read the Bible or other spiritual book to gain insight. The seagull's white color symbolizes peace—now is a good time to make peace with an old enemy or relative you never liked; to make this easier, carry a seagull feather with you.

SPARROW: The unassuming sparrow's happy hopping reminds us that we don't need to be beautiful or rich to have a happy life. Being attracted to this bird means you should take more pleasure in the simple things, and not overthink your problems. Seeing a dead sparrow is a portent of bad luck, so be extra careful in traffic if you come across one! Seeing a sparrow on a Thursday means you'll have success at work or find a new job soon.

STARLING: Being a talking bird, the starling helps you to speak out against injustice or speak up for yourself or loved one. This goes back to the story in the *Mabinogion* (a book of old Welsh tales) about Branwen, who was married to the King of Ireland who abused her. Branwen taught a starling to talk and sent it to her brother, Bran the Blessed, who came to save her. A starling is also a sign that you should look further into your future, maybe by scrying or reading tarot.

CHAPTER 4

Well-being for Witches

From romance and friendship to family and neighbors,
the following pages are packed with simple ways to boost
love and well-being in your relationships and, most
importantly, for yourself.

Love and romance

A little romance works wonders for your well-being. Whether you are looking for a special someone or hope to strengthen the love bonds between you and your partner, there are plenty of ways to bring love magic into your life.

BEFORE YOU BEGIN

As with all magic that involves others, but especially when it comes to love witchery, it is important to remember the Wiccan Rede: "And it harm none, do as thou wilt!" This basically means you can do what you wish, as long as it doesn't harm others or go against their freewill. For example, it would be considered black magic to force someone to fall in love with you or to stay with you against their wishes. However, you absolutely *can* do magic that helps someone notice you, or encourages any loving feelings that are already there but may be lying dormant.

ATTRACTING LOVE WITH ROSE QUARTZ

To attract love, I recommend wearing a round rose quartz. To strengthen its power, wear it on a chain next to your skin, ideally at the level of your heart. If you are specifically trying to attract a man, use a gold chain because gold represents the Sun God and male energy. Alternatively, carry a piece of rose quartz in your pocket, or wear a ring with an oval- or heart-shaped rose quartz set into it.

Before you go out, while wearing your rose quartz, spray a cloud of vanilla- or cinnamon-based scent in front of you. Take a step forward into the scent while saying: "Love comes to me, I am stepping into my loving future!" Rubbing the rose quartz with cinnamon oil will also enhance your loving energy.

MAGIC MAKEUP

Makeup isn't just to freshen up your face, it can be a form of magic too. Keep your makeup with rose quartz or a bunch of pink and red flowers to increase its loving energies before you use it.

BLUSH: Choose pink blush for romantic love.

NAIL POLISH: Wear red nail polish for passion.

FOUNDATION: Apply foundation to your face in the shape of a heart before blending it in.

BODY SPRAY: Draw a sigil on yourself using body spray in a shape that symbolizes love to you.

PRACTICAL MAGIC **BEWITCHING BRACELET**

Try this magical bracelet charm using pink and red ribbons to help you find love.

1 Choose two ribbons, one pink and one red, each long enough to make a bracelet.

2 Twirl them around each other and rub a fragrant rose petal, or some rose oil), onto the ribbons.

3 Think about the type of partner you are trying to attract. What are the three to five most important qualities that they must have? Make a knot in the twirled ribbon for each of these qualities.

4 Tie the finished bracelet around your left wrist, because the left is associated with intuition and emotion.

5 You can add a little pendant, such as a rose quartz heart, or two silver turtle doves (a symbol of love) if you like, to bring extra power to this spell.

6 Keep the bracelet on your wrist until you have found love.

FINDING LOVE AT WORK

If you're hoping you might become more than just co-workers with a special someone at work, try these ideas to help love find its way to you.

- Keep a photo of happy people, such as your children or parents, in a heart-shaped frame on your desk.

- Dress in bright pink (the color of romantic love), or at least add a pink accent to your outfit, like a pink purse, scarf, or rose quartz jewelry.

- Use a stone with a red heart on it as a paperweight.

- Use a red stapler, especially if your potential love interest gives you papers to work on.

- Take heart-shaped cookies or pink lemonade into work. Make sure you offer some personally to your love interest.

PRACTICAL MAGIC **FIND A LOVE THAT GROWS**

Draw on Mother Nature's magical powers when finding love. Bonus points if you start this ritual for romance on the new moon!

1 Write your intentions or dedication to finding love onto a terracotta pot using chalk.

2 Half-fill the pot with soil.

3 Collect biodegradable items that you think will help to summon a lover, such as rose petals for romance, grapes or vine leaves for indulgence, or oak bark or chips for masculinity. You could also write down your desires on pink paper (for romance) or red paper (for passion).

4 Put the items into the pot and place more soil on top.

5 Pick out an appropriate seed (such as apple, peach, nectarine, or grape) or a rose cutting, and plant it in the soil.

6 Place the pot in a south-facing window or outside, then water it and tend to it. As the plant grows, so will your love prospects.

KEEPING THE ROMANCE ALIVE

Before going on a date, or to strengthen the bonds in your current relationship, try these powerful love boosters.

• Take a bath with rose-scented bath bubbles or add a few drops of rose oil to your bath.

• Try a short meditation to make you more self-confident and able to open yourself up to love—visualize love gods and goddesses such as Eros, Aphrodite, Cupid, Isis, and Venus in a circle around you, giving you strength. Then see yourself with your love, both smiling and happy together.

• Put a plastic snake under the bed to encourage more fun in the bedroom.

• If you and your partner are both into magic, jump over a bonfire or red candle placed toward the south side of your home. Make sure it is on a sturdy surface and otherwise safe! This will bless you both with the passion and fierceness of the element of fire for your activities in the bedroom later.

• Massage or rub each other with oils that encourage passion, such as almond oil with a little cinnamon.

FOODS OF LOVE

Embrace the loving magic that can be found within everyday food items.

• Eating foods that are phallic in shape, such as carrots, cucumbers, bananas, and ginger, is an easy way to increase the passion between you and your partner. Serve the food whole or cut it up when preparing your meal.

• To encourage a gentle, romantic love, make your partner a raspberry-based fruit punch, chocolate raspberry tart, or other raspberry-based dish, and add cinnamon for magical passion. As you prepare it, stir the ingredients clockwise and chant nine times: "I seek love as below, so above." You could also throw a couple of handfuls of raspberry leaves into a warm bath and submerge yourself fully nine times while saying the same chant.

• For those needing help with libido issues, women can try drinking a glass of milk, which represents the Moon Goddess and femininity, every day and men can eat an orange fruit or vegetable, such as an orange or a carrot, as this represents the Sun God, energy, and virility.

DATE NIGHT IDEAS

LIGHT a candle as a beacon for love to come to you.

DRINK red wine for passionate love or rosé for romantic love.

DECORATE the table with red and pink flowers, which symbolize love.

EAT some cream with your dessert for the pure love of the Mother Goddess.

PRACTICAL MAGIC **DREAM DECISIONS**

If you have two or more potential partners interested in you and need help deciding between them, try this simple ritual before bed. You will need two or more pink pieces of paper (or red, if the sexual partnership is most important to you) and a blue pen, for wisdom and insight.

1 Write the name of one love interest on a piece of paper, as well as their five best and worst qualities.

2 Repeat with another piece of paper for another love interest (and keep going if there are more).

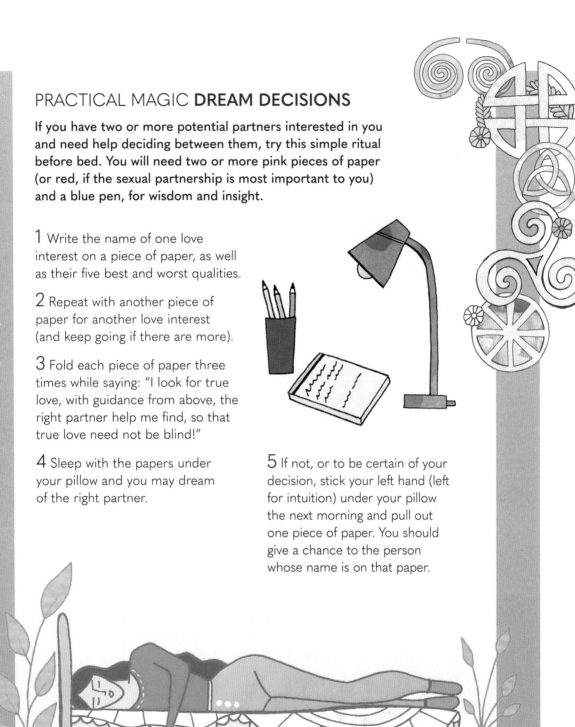

3 Fold each piece of paper three times while saying: "I look for true love, with guidance from above, the right partner help me find, so that true love need not be blind!"

4 Sleep with the papers under your pillow and you may dream of the right partner.

5 If not, or to be certain of your decision, stick your left hand (left for intuition) under your pillow the next morning and pull out one piece of paper. You should give a chance to the person whose name is on that paper.

LETTING GO OF A RELATIONSHIP

Is your relationship over? The most important thing
is to be gentle with yourself. Go for a walk during the
day so the Sun God can warm your heart again and
give you the strength to carry on. A walk in the
moonlight will allow the Moon Goddess to envelop
you in her love and compassion.

Try the Cut the Cord ritual (see box below)
when you feel ready.

To help you look forward to a positive future, wear a clear
quartz crystal against your skin, close to your heart. This will
give you more energy and invite positive people into your life.

PRACTICAL MAGIC **CUT THE CORD**

This gentle ritual will help you to break the bonds that tie
you to relationships that no longer serve you.

1 Sit quietly in the
middle of a room.

2 Imagine the other
person is sitting opposite
you and you are linked
by a silver cord.

3 Think about all the
experiences you had
together, good and bad.
Cry and laugh if you
want to and take as
long as you need.

4 When you feel ready,
symbolically cut the silver
cord between you with
a real pair of scissors.

5 As you do this, say:
"In love and light, I let
you go" three times.

6 Repeat this ritual
once a week until you
feel better.

Friendships

Nothing boosts our well-being quite like a chat with a close confidante or a night out with a group of close friends. So it is important to build strong connections with others and create supportive friendships in your life.

THE POWER OF YELLOW

Yellow is the color of friendship. To encourage new or stronger friendships, wear something yellow (even if it's just yellow underwear!) when you go to your sports club, the market, a friend's party, or anywhere else you are hoping to make or improve friendships.

If you find it difficult to approach others, perhaps because you are shy, you can also light a yellow candle on a waxing moon. As the moon's size increases in the sky, so will your circle of friends. With the candle lit, visualize having fun with new friends and chant:

I am a bit meek,

But friendship I seek.

Happiness and fun,

Will be drawn to me by Father Sun.

You can also try the chant above while out and about. Simply chant, under your breath if necessary, while feeling the sun's warmth and support on you.

PRACTICAL MAGIC **FRIEND FINDER DIVINATION**

Find out how to make new friends with this easy divination. You will need a yellow candle and a bowl of cold water. You can use the same yellow candle from the spell on page 87, or a separate candle—one spell is not dependent on the other.

1 Light the candle and gaze into the flame.

2 Think about how you want to make new friends and ask the God and Goddess to guide you.

3 When you feel ready, quickly turn the candle upside down and let the wax drip into the bowl of water.

4 Look at the shapes the blobs of wax make in the water. From this, divine what is the best way to make new friends. For example, a blob may

look like a dog, suggesting you could make new friends when walking your dog or volunteering for a dog rescue. Or if there is a blob on the side of the bowl closest to your home office, this could be a sign to put more effort into making friends at work.

PRACTICAL MAGIC **FORGET ME NOT**

Encourage contact from a friend who you haven't heard from in a while.

1 Address a white envelope with your friend's details. If you don't have their full physical address, simply write "[Name's] address" along with the town and country, if you know that.

2 Write a short, heartfelt note about how you miss them and hope they are well and feel able to contact you soon. Place the note in the envelope and seal it with a kiss.

3 Burn it in your fireplace, in a fire outside, or even just use a lighter to burn it.

4 As the envelope goes up in smoke, visualize that smoke traveling on the winds to wherever your friend is.

SOOTHING TROUBLED WATERS

If you are having trouble with a friend—perhaps you have had a disagreement or there is a negative person in your friend group—try these soothing spells.

• Use peppermint soap to wash your hands before meeting your troublesome friend, or wear a couple of drops of peppermint oil on a cloth when meeting, to help clear the air.

• To diffuse an argument you have had with a friend, roll up a photo of the two of you happy together and tie a white ribbon around it, making three knots—one for the argument, and two more to represent the two of you. On the next new moon (the time for new beginnings), take a deep breath and undo the three knots, visualizing peace and happiness once again. Then contact your friend in whichever way you normally do.

• If a friend is too intense, and you need them to calm down, or you just need a break from them, find an item that symbolizes your friend, such as a photo of them, a picture of their favorite animal, or a piece of their favorite fruit. Then submerge the item fully in water while you think of their hold on you lessening. Put the item in your fridge to chill, literally and metaphorically.

• If a friend has been bad at contacting you, they may just need some space due to their own issues. But to encourage your friend to reach out to you, first write their name in yellow on a piece of paper or find a photo of the two of you happy together. Then place the paper or photo under your phone or computer (whichever method of communication you normally use with them)—you might hear from them soon.

THE POWER OF THREE

To remove toxic behavior or a toxic friend from your life, write the issue or name of the friend in black ink on a white piece of toilet paper. Black symbolizes the negativity while white represents peace and will help to neutralize the negative energy. Hold the toilet paper in both hands and spend some time visualizing all your stress and bad feelings flowing into the paper. Then fold it three times and say: "By the power of three, I let it be. By the power of three, a peaceful future I see!" Finally, flush the toilet paper down the toilet.

If you have a friend who keeps annoying you or putting you down, it is always useful to remember the Wiccan Law of Three: "Anything you do reflects three times onto you." This is utilized in the Reflection Ritual (see box below).

PRACTICAL MAGIC **REFLECTION RITUAL**

If a friend is gossiping about you, try this mirror magic. You will need a small mirror. Any shape will do but I recommend triangular, as this will increase the effects of the spell due to the Law of Three.

1 Add a drop of clove oil to the surface of the mirror.

2 Rub it counterclockwise while saying: "I am positive and strong, this negativity is wrong. Anything you do reflects three times back onto you!"

3 Repeat step 2 as many times as you like, but I recommend nine times (three times three).

4 If you know who the gossip is, set the mirror up to face them. The mirror can be hidden if necessary, perhaps in your bag or concealed somewhere in the room.

5 If you are less sure who the gossip is, you could sew the mirror into your coat or another piece of clothing you wear often, reflective side facing out.

Family

Most of us love our families, but sometimes the closeness can cause trouble, especially if you have different political or religious views.

BRING PEACE AND DISPEL NEGATIVITY

There are many ways you can cleanse your home of negative energy to ease tension, bring peace, and make a fresh start after any family struggles.

If you have children who don't get along, try this quick chant while visualizing the siblings having fun together:

The sibling rivalry between these two,

Must cease now, they must be true

Siblings to one another,

Treat each other well and not be a bother.

Caring, loving friends they'll be,

Siblings filled with harmony.

And so it shall be!

You can also use color magic to help your children get along. Try decorating the living room with a blue throw (for healing), buy a white ball (for peace) that they can play with together, or serve them yellow foods or candy (for friendship) that they can enjoy together.

PRACTICAL MAGIC **PEPPERMINT POTION**

Try this easy spell to ease tension between family members.

1 Brew some peppermint tea, preferably with fresh leaves. Add a spoonful of honey, stirring clockwise.

2 Walk around the house with the tea, letting the steam waft into every corner, especially into areas where arguments have happened. The peppermint will clear negative energy and the honey will leave a sweet blessing of harmony.

3 When you have finished, drink the tea, preferably sharing it with the rest of the family.

PRACTICAL MAGIC **RESTORE THE PEACE**

This simple charm can help to make a family member more peaceful.

1 Write the name of the family member on a white piece of paper.

2 Light a white candle and think of practical ways you can help bring calm to the relationship.

3 Look into the candle flame and visualize it burning away any negativity or past regrets in the relationship.

4 When you are ready, drip candle wax onto their name until it is completely covered in pure white candle wax.

5 Keep the paper safe until the relationship is healed, then bury it in some soil.

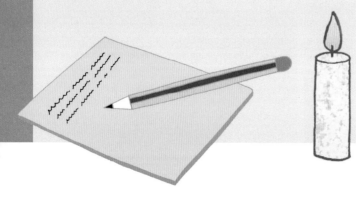

FAMILY PROTECTION

To keep your family together and safe, or to protect a family member
from gossip, bullying, or at a time of crisis, try these easy spells:

• Place an ivy houseplant in the west corner of your home to harness the healing power of the water element.

• If a family member is in crisis, visualize them in a glowing pentagram, happy and healthy, so that the four elements (earth, air, fire, water) and spirit may all protect them and keep them safe.

• If your child is being bullied, make a figure out of clay that represents them. You can scratch their name on it, too. Rub the figure with clove oil or surround it with a few cloves to remove negativity, and wrap it in white cotton wool, which represents peace and positive energy. Keep the figure somewhere safe.

• If you need to contact someone, such as the school or a neighbor, about an issue with your child, do it between the half hour and the full hour when the hands of the clock will be moving "upward" as you talk, which means that things will start to look up for your child.

PRACTICAL MAGIC **PROTECTIVE INTENTION SPELL**

Harness the power of positive intentions with this simple protection spell.

1 Light a black candle and circle it with salt, preferably black salt if you have it or can make it.

2 Think about your intentions to protect your family against negative energies and misfortune. Write them down on a piece of paper.

3 Envision the intentions already fulfilled. Imagine the family home as a place with positive vibes and nothing but growth and happiness.

4 Burn the paper in the flame of the candle when you're done.

5 After a few minutes, snuff out the candle gently instead of blowing it out. Watch the smoke disperse, visualizing the bad energy disappearing with it.

Neighbors

Communication is the best magic when it comes to dealing with neighbors. You could be really annoyed with your neighbor, but remember, they may have reasons for what they are doing, or not doing! Unless you are truly afraid for your safety, talk to them first.

FIND HARMONY WITH YOUR NEIGHBORS

When talking to your neighbors, wear white for peace or blue for calmness and wisdom. To invoke friendship and harmony with neighbors you have trouble with, each Friday, face in the direction of the neighbors and say this blessing: "Strife and trouble may cease, all we want is peace!" You can repeat this before meeting them, too. You could also make them some cookies—the sugar in the cookies represents the sweetness of a good relationship, and adding lemon will neutralize sourness and encourage friendship.

BOUNDARIES AND PROTECTION

If talking to your neighbors is not helping the issue, try these magical tips and tricks in and around your home.

• Put a barrier up, literally. This could be a fence (wooden for the blessing of Mother Earth, white for peace, or black to neutralize negativity), or a natural barrier such as a thorny bush or roses. You can also gather some white feathers and tie them to fence posts to bring peace in.

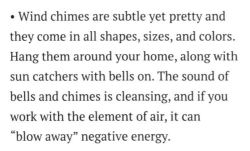

• Wind chimes are subtle yet pretty and they come in all shapes, sizes, and colors. Hang them around your home, along with sun catchers with bells on. The sound of bells and chimes is cleansing, and if you work with the element of air, it can "blow away" negative energy.

• Hang horseshoes over each door (points facing upward). Good fortune and nice neighbors will "collect" inside the U of the horseshoe while bad neighbors will be symbolically walked away.

• Place a small, discreet mirror on the outside of your front door, or on the wall behind your headboard if you have neighbors on the other side of your bedroom wall. The mirror will reflect and bounce any negativity sent your way back to where it came from.

• Make an arrow shape out of small, potted plants in your window, with the arrow pointing outward to keep annoying neighbors away and discourage them from visiting. Or plant flowers in your garden in an arrow shape pointing toward your house to encourage nice neighbors.

• If you are bad with plants, you could make an arrow using chopped herbs or protective oil, such as clove, chamomile, and nutmeg, on your floorboards or the sidewalk outside.

• My favorite way to deter bad neighbors and any local troublesome teens is to make a paste to repel them. You can always say it is to discourage slugs, if asked. Mix together four tablespoons of coarse salt, one tablespoon of ground black pepper, and 11 cloves, then add vinegar to make a thick paste. Put some of this along the boundary line between the two properties or between your home and the street.

EASE THEM OUT OF YOUR LIFE

If your neighbors are not super bad people but you just don't get along, try setting them up with a fantastic opportunity that takes them far away, rather than forcing them out aggressively. To do this successfully, you'd need to know some information about them, such as where their wider family lives (who they may want to move closer to), or what kind of job they might be looking for. Then perform a love spell, family spell, or job spell with them in mind, to distance them from your life with love and kindness.

Taking care of yourself

As a witch, you will not have your full power unless you look after yourself. Thankfully, there are plenty of ways to nurture and nourish the most important relationship in your life—your relationship with yourself!

BE YOUR BEST SELF

Try these simple ideas to enhance your own personal witchy wellness.

• Wearing your favorite perfume is an easy way to bring happiness and positive feelings to your day. Or choose a perfume that suits your intention for the day, such as vanilla for friendship and calmness, rose to attract love, or lavender to calm you if it will be a stressful day. You can also be intentional with the drinks you choose (see box below).

• Wear an evil eye amulet to draw evil eyes away from you, or a hamsa for protection and good luck.

• If you have bad habits you want to get rid of, write them down in black ink on a white piece of paper. Submerge the paper in a container of water and place it at the back of the freezer to freeze out your bad habits.

INTENTIONAL TEAS AND OTHER DRINKS

Use both the smell and the magical meaning of a drink to bring intention into your day.

SWEET TEA: A reminder of the sweetness of life.

ROSEHIP TEA: To encourage self-love.

CHAMOMILE TEA: Restores calm.

BLACK TEA WITH MILK (OR JUST MILK): For peace and general positive energy.

BLUEBERRY LEMONADE: For wisdom.

ORANGE JUICE: For justice.

ALE: To receive the blessing of your ancestors.

HARNESS THE MOON

Turn to the power of the moon to discover your inner goddess and embrace all the qualities that make you, you.

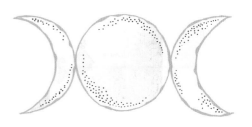

• Moonstone is a great stone for women to wear to balance out female energies, especially if you are having menstruation issues. It also brings out your inner feminine and gains you the protection of the Maiden, Mother, and Crone Goddesses.

• To become more self-confident and bring out your inner Moon Goddess, rub a jasmine flower (or drop of jasmine essential oil, or perfume) on your third eye chakra while chanting: "I am a Goddess, I am great! Divine love is my fate. With the guidance of the moon, happy and successful I'll be soon."

• If you would like to seek the help and blessing of the deities, you can make magical moon water. Leave clean water (preferably from a natural source but tap water will do) outside under a full moon. Then store it in the fridge and visualize the love, protection, and guidance of the Moon Goddess entering you whenever you drink from it.

PRACTICAL MAGIC
INNER GODDESS MEDITATION

Seek guidance from your inner goddess with this meditation to gain more peace and calm in your life.

1 Sit somewhere quiet and comfortable. You can even lay on your bed as long as you won't fall asleep.

2 Slow your breathing down. Concentrate on each arm and leg in turn, getting them to relax, then your torso and finally your head.

3 Close your eyes and visualize a beautifully ornate mirror. Look into the mirror at yourself.

4 Ask for your inner goddess to come and show herself to you. If you already have a favorite goddess, you can visualize her. If not, be open—it may be any goddess that you have read about, a departed loved one you admire, or even an idealized version of yourself.

5 When you "see" your inner goddess, thank her for coming and ask her for any wisdom she may wish to impart; this could be general advice, specific suggestions about a problem you face, or tips for the future.

6 When you feel you have talked enough with your inner goddess, thank her for coming.

7 Then bring your concentration back to your body. First your head, then your torso, then each arm and leg, before opening your eyes.

POSITIVE AFFIRMATIONS

You can use mirror magic to boost your confidence by creating a mantra that you say every morning as you get ready for work or school. This mantra should be personal to you, depending on what aspect of your personality you want to work on, but here are three suggestions:

I can do this, I will do this, doing it will bring me bliss!

I am a good person, but I am also a strong person. No one will walk over me.

*I love myself, and the world loves me.
By the power of three, so mote it be!*

You can easily repeat your mantra throughout the day, in the bathroom at work or school, or just before a date in the evening. Here are some other simple ways to incorporate positive affirmations into your daily life:

• Place a small mirror inside a pendant or a locket, and hold it with your thumb and forefinger while repeating your personal mantra in your head.

• Think of a positive affirmation about yourself (such as "I am lovable and a hard worker!"). Write it out by hand a hundred times without interruption. After a while it will become second nature, working its magic to become true in your subconscious.

• Make an affirmation jar (see box on next page).

PRACTICAL MAGIC **AFFIRMATION JAR**

A witchy yet discreet spell is to make an affirmation jar full of positive energy!

1 Get a small, clean jam jar or bottle.

2 Think of some positive affirmations about yourself such as "I look and feel good!" and write them down on small pieces of paper. Put them in the jar.

3 Add a clear quartz to gain pure, positive energy, then fill the container with clean soil to help you stay grounded, or with rice to multiply the truth of the affirmations inside.

4 Carry the jar with you or keep it on your altar. Shake it if you need a little boost.

CALMING AND UPLIFTING CHANTS

If you are anxious, take three deep breaths and say: "When I finish counting ten to one, my anxiety will be gone!" Then count backward from ten. Take another three deep breaths when you reach one.

If you are stressed, sprinkle dried chamomile or jasmine flowers in a circle around the source of your stress. For example, around your bed if your sleep is affected, or around your desk if work is the cause of your stress. Chant five times: "Peace and contentment come to me, stress and negativity, let me be!"

The old Celtic nursery rhyme below can be used as a quick chant when you are feeling down. Afterward, do a little hop and dance—be silly and make yourself laugh to feel happy again!

Ride a cockhorse to Banbury Cross,

To see a fine lady upon a white horse,

With rings on her fingers and bells on her toes,

She shall have music wherever she goes.

CHAPTER 5

Your Witchy Schedule

Witches often practice certain magic depending on the time of day or day of the week, as these have different magical energies that help spells succeed. This chapter includes everyday magic for every day, and every time!

Magical mornings

How we start our day can set the tone for what follows, so making a few magical adjustments to your morning routine can work wonders for welcoming in positivity, luck, and success.

DAWN

Dawn (like dusk, see page 111) is an important time of day because it is a time "between the worlds" where the Moon Goddess and the Sun God meet.

• To make the most of the dawn's magical energy, go somewhere you can see the sun come up, ideally where you can have your feet on the earth. If that is not possible, look out the window in the direction of the rising sun. To give an already magical food or piece of jewelry or clothing that extra bit of magical energy, hold the item in front of you and ask the Mother Earth and the Sun God, who is coming into his power, to bless the item. As the sun comes up, raise the item up over your head.

• Dawn is also a great time for money magic. Go to your garden or a park with some birdseed at dawn, and, as you watch the sun come up, think of the reason you need money and what you will do with it. Sprinkle the seeds around you clockwise and say nine times: "My need be the seed and it harm none, my will be done!" As always, money magic works better when you are realistic with your financial goal!

• Do you need a specific amount of money to buy a home, pay off a debt, or get that present your child really wants? Etch the amount you need on a green candle then light it for a few minutes every day at dawn. Every time the sun rises, so will your monetary luck, until you receive the amount you need.

PRACTICAL MAGIC **DAWN DIVINATION**

Dawn is a good time for meditation. It tends to be quiet and easier to access spirits, deities, and your inner self.

1 Go to a natural source of water such as a river, the sea, or even a pond.

2 Look out onto the water and talk to the sun (and the moon, if visible). Ask them to show you the answer to a question you have, a solution to a problem, or to grant you a glimpse of your future.

3 Watch the ripples of the water, or the waves coming in if there are any, and visualize the element of water bringing you inspiration and the answer to your problems. As you watch the surface of the sea, wait for a symbol or clue to appear.

4 If nothing comes, try closing your eyes and asking the water to send you a sign in your mind's eye.

WAKE UP TO WONDERFUL THINGS

When you wake up, don't get up immediately. Instead, take a few deep breaths and stretch. Smile, and think of something good that *will* happen today. It can be something as small as having your favorite cereal for breakfast, meeting a friend for lunch, or your favorite television show being on in the evening. Then think of something good that you *want* to happen, but is not certain, like a promotion, hoping to see your crush on the bus, or an old friend getting in touch. The positive energy and happiness from the first thought will mingle with the second and make it more likely to happen.

PRACTICAL MAGIC **INTENTIONAL INCANTATIONS**

If you have a specific goal in mind, this charm using a carnelian stone works especially well if you start it just after a new moon. Repeat it after each new moon until you are well on the way to reaching your goal.

1 Get up just before dawn to see the sunrise. If the weather is overcast, or your window doesn't face that way, just look in the direction of the sunrise.

2 Hold the carnelian stone in your hands.

3 In your own words, pray to the Lord and Lady (or your patron deities if you have any) for help in making your new project, goal, or desire happen.

BEWITCHING BIRDS

Did you know that birds can offer omens and magical messages about the future?

Put birdseed out at night, then look out your window first thing the next morning. The first bird you see will symbolize something about your day (see box, right).

If you have a question about a specific issue, choose birdseed suited to the problem. For example, use corn for a friendship issue (yellow stands for friendship), sunflower seeds for questions about men (the sun represents male energy), pumpkin seeds for justice (pumpkins are orange, the color of justice), or golden sultanas for money issues (golden colors symbolize money).

THE MAGICAL MEANINGS OF BIRDS

Birds can offer hints for how to go about your day.

BLACKBIRD: Do something spiritual today.

BLUE TIT: Be careful with your health today.

RAVEN: Remember a departed loved one.

ROBIN: Love will come your way.

SEAGULL: Make peace with someone you have argued with.

MIRROR, MIRROR

As you brush your teeth or do your makeup, look in the mirror
and chant this three times to make your day better!

I am a good person,

I am beautiful,

I deserve to be happy,

I deserve to be loved,

*I deserve to be comfortable—financially,
mentally, physically, and emotionally.*

PRACTICAL MAGIC **SHOWER SPELL**

The shower is a wonderful place for magic. Use a peppermint shampoo to
bring fresh thoughts and financial success, or lavender body wash to calm
you before a busy and stressful day. You can also make your own magical
pomander to hang on your showerhead.

1 Gather the materials
you need for the
pomander:

• To improve health, try a
blue cloth (for healing)
and add chamomile
flowers, aloe vera, and
a clear quartz crystal.

• To improve your
financial situation, get
a gold or white cloth,
add gold ribbon, a piece
of ginger, a clean coin,
and some basil.

• To help find love, add
some rose water or rose
petals, a rose quartz,
cinnamon stick, and
some red pepper flakes
to a red cloth.

2 Tie all the ingredients
up in the cloth and fasten
it on your showerhead so
the water flows through it.

3 Once the water is
warm, step into the
shower. As you do so,
visualize stepping into a
new day and a new start
for anything that went
wrong the day before.

Magical days

Much of the everyday magic that can be done during the daytime is found throughout this book, but there are also some spells that are especially good to do at specific times during the daylight hours.

LUNCHTIME

Lunchtime is a great time to take a quick study break to grow your spirituality and witchiness. Read a book like this one, read your tarot cards, practice guided meditation with your headphones on, or go for a walk to get in touch with Mother Nature.

A simple lunchtime meditation can reduce your stress and recycle it as energy for your work and daily chores. Sit comfortably, breathe deeply, and feel your body relax. Visualize a bubble of blue healing light all around you. If you have extra time to relax fully, "build up" the bubble in layers to make it extra strong, and "feel the heal."

Be sure to eat something that will sustain you for the rest of your errands or work, and that gets you in touch with deities that can guide you. For example:

- Grains (a quinoa bowl, rice, or even just a piece of bread) to symbolize the deities showing you the way to abundance.

- An orange, warmed by the sun before you eat it, for justice and the strength of the Sun God.

- A piece of fruit, some vegetables, brown chocolate, or coffee to get you in touch with Mother Nature.

- Yogurt or cream cheese (white foods) to gain the blessing of the Moon Goddess and find peace in your day.

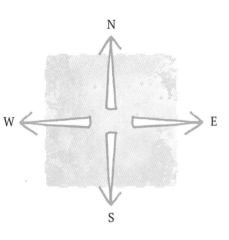

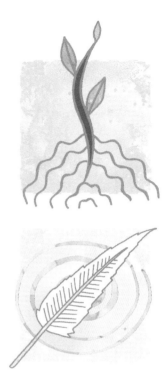

COMBATTING NEGATIVITY

If you are having trouble with someone you mostly see during the daytime, like a co-worker, a friend you see at lunch, or similar, try this charm. Write their name on white paper with blue ink, or use a photograph, and lean it against a blue candle (for wisdom and truth). Light the candle and say the following three times:

Earth of the north, nourish the truth,

Three times three, set me free, set me free.

Wind in the east, clear the air,

Three times three, let me see, let me see.

Fires in the south, burn the lies,

Three times three, set me free, set me free,

Water of the west, cleanse, let lies rest,

Three times three, let me see, let me see.

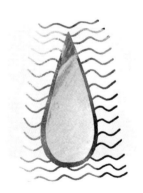

Repeat this spell at least once a week until you feel no more negative emotions from or toward the person.

PRACTICAL MAGIC **TEACUP DIVINATION**

If you are confused about an issue, try this quick divination that you can do in a teacup just as easily as a cauldron, depending on where you are. You will need a herb that is suitable for what you need to know, for example, basil for money issues, peppermint to find the reason behind a fight, or cinnamon for love.

1 Pour water into a mug.

2 Add a large pinch of your chosen herb to the mug. If you don't have any herbs, use whatever is nearby—crush a dry leaf, use pencil shavings, or similar.

3 Dip your left index finger into the water, stirring slowly while saying (in your head if in public): "Lord and Lady be on my side, let me see what others may hide!"

Magical evenings and nights

In the past, nighttime was when witches traditionally met because few people were about, and it was easier to hide at a time when this was still necessary. Still, now, most covens meet in the evening so we can marvel at the beauty of the moon, but also because, on a practical level, that is when most people are free from work and family obligations.

DUSK

Just like dawn (see page 104), dusk is an important time of day. To remove any negative thoughts you've had during the day, light a fire in your fireplace or garden at dusk. Write your problems or any negative gossip or rumors you have heard onto a piece of paper with a black pen (for negativity). Fold the paper three times, each time saying the words below. Then, toss the paper into the fire.

Gossip, slander, nasty people out,

With this spell, I cast you out!

I toss their words into the fires,

They will clearly be seen as liars.

All the evil that they say,

Make it all go away!

If you need help with a troubling obstacle to your career path, or an annoying person, try this chant: "As the sun sets this day I name, Lord and Lady, remove this bane!"

PRACTICAL MAGIC **OLD KEY**

Try this spell at dusk if you need a new place to live or are not sure if you should move. You will need an old key. It should not be from your own home. Ideally, you don't know what the key unlocks (you could get one from a flea market or ask a friend to give you one).

1 Hold the key between your flat palms. Close your eyes, relax, and slow your breathing.

2 For a few minutes, think about your ideal home, but be realistic!

3 Repeat once a week.

4 With time, your thoughts will solidify into a concrete list of requirements and a definite area where you want to live.

PREPARE TO PARTY

If you are going out in the evening (to a party, perhaps) and want to look your best, dedicate your makeup to the Moon Goddess and ask her to lend you her beauty.

Place new makeup purchases on a windowsill where the moon can shine on it. Say: "Beautiful Goddess of the Moon I ask, lend me your beauty, soon! For your radiance I ask, in your love I bask."

PRACTICAL MAGIC **FLUSH AWAY BAD HABITS**

Perform this ritual in your bathroom once it is completely dark. You will need a few squares of toilet paper, a pen, a black candle, and a white candle.

1 Light a black candle to absorb negativity.

2 On each square of toilet paper, write one bad habit or guilt you carry.

3 Light a white candle to send purifying light to your mind and soul, and peace to your heart.

4 Drop each square of paper into the toilet, watch it get soaked, then flush it away, while saying: "Here are my bad habits, my guilt and my shame, as the paper flows down, so too goes my stain."

5 As the paper is flushed away, send any feelings of guilt down the toilet with it.

6 Repeat this spell as often as needed.

7 Blow the candles out but keep them specifically for repeating this spell.

WASH AWAY THE DAY

The bathroom is useful for lots of magic, especially for getting rid of bad habits. When you are in the shower or bathtub after a long day, rub your hands with a bar of soap or a washcloth counterclockwise to remove stress and negativity. Then watch the water disappear down the drain, leaving you cleansed, magically and physically.

A GOOD NIGHT'S SLEEP

Sleep is so important! Lack of it can negatively affect your physical and mental health, so having a good bedtime routine is crucial. Make sure to slow down about an hour before bed, minimize your use of electronics, and keep bedroom lights low. These magical sleep rituals can also help:

• To calm down in the evening, make a small cup of warm milk with honey. The whiteness of the milk stands for peace and calm, as well as the protection of the Moon Goddess. The honey represents the sweetness of a good night's sleep and reminds you of the good things that happened during the day. Stir the honey in clockwise and say: "Sleep now come, heaven it is from. May I sleep long and well, until the morning alarm bell!"

• Drink a cup of vervain or chamomile tea each evening, about 30 minutes before bed. Stir a spoonful of honey in, first counterclockwise while you imagine all the worries and stresses of your day leaving you, then clockwise, as you think of a good night's sleep and positive things that are going to happen tomorrow.

• Get a pale blue piece of cloth and fold it up with lavender and chamomile blossoms (essential oils work too). Call on the goddess Pasithea, Greek goddess of rest, to watch over your sleep. Sit or lay comfortably, slow your breathing, and say: "Stress goes away, worries vanish! Bad energy I banish! I lay down to sleep, it will be restful and deep!" Then place the cloth under your pillow.

• If you are having nightmares, sprinkle a circle of dried rosemary around the bed. This protects your spirit during sleep and keeps nightmares away.

SLEEP LIKE A BABY

Does your child suffer from night terrors? Check in on them after they are asleep. Visualize them in a bubble of blue, protective, healing light, then whisper:

Health and happy my children may be,

They mean the earth and the sky to me.

So Sun God and Goddess of the Moon,

Please let them sleep tight, and not wake up too soon!

Days of the week

Every day of the week is ruled by a specific god or planet—they can bring extra power to magic worked on that day, or can make magic resolve differently, depending on which day of the week it is done. For example, love magic is traditionally done on a Friday, the day of love goddess Venus.

MONDAY

The name Monday comes from "moon's day," making it a great day to harness the moon's energy.

- Practice magic involving emotions.

- Ask the Moon Goddess for her blessing.

- Practice "girl power" magic for self-confidence.

- Wear silver and moonstones to bring you closer to the divine feminine.

- Make your silver jewelry magical by leaving it out in the moonlight.

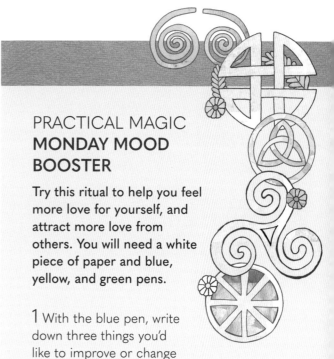

PRACTICAL MAGIC
MONDAY MOOD BOOSTER

Try this ritual to help you feel more love for yourself, and attract more love from others. You will need a white piece of paper and blue, yellow, and green pens.

1 With the blue pen, write down three things you'd like to improve or change about yourself.

2 With the yellow pen, write down six things you like about yourself.

3 With the green pen, write down nine compliments that you have received from others. It may take some time and be a bit embarrassing to do this, but trust me, you will find nine things and if not, ask people!

4 Fold the paper three times: once to remove negativity, once to remind yourself of your blessings, and once to invite love into your life (including self-love) and store it somewhere safe.

5 Take the paper out and read it whenever you feel low.

TUESDAY

Tuesday is the day of Mars—both the planet and the god of lust, action, bravery, courage, and purification. This is a good day to practice magic that will help you reach your goals and make yourself seen, so wear strong, bold colors like bright red, and neon colors. Dress to impress and turn heads!

In my training coven, we called this day "Tarot Tuesday." I encourage you to do a tarot spread to spot any issues you need to know about.

Tuesday is also a good day for a justice spell. That doesn't necessarily mean the law will go in your favor or the police will arrest a perpetrator, but that the universe will bring you justice. On a Tuesday, inscribe a wrongdoer's name on an orange candle and light it for a few minutes while chanting the words below three times. Continue this weekly until the issue is solved.

I seek justice for me,

At peace I want to be,

Please show [name] what they do is wrong,

Help me find true justice and where I belong.

WEDNESDAY

Wednesday, being "hump day," is a good time to take stock of your week and your recent actions. Wednesday is associated with the god of wisdom, Odin, and planet Mercury. It is a good day to inspire new projects or to deepen your occult and witchy knowledge. Wear purple, pentagrams, and feathers to bring inspiration on the wind.

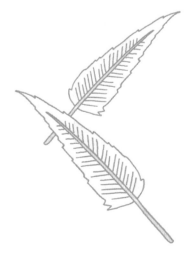

Wednesday is also the day best for communication rituals:

• Schedule any difficult meetings or discussions with your partner on a Wednesday, as you are more likely to come to an understanding.

• Light a white candle, or position a covert white pentagram nearby (as a wall decoration, worn as jewelry, or made with white pens) to increase peaceful energies.

• Visualize the four elements to ensure a balanced argument.

• To help you see the true nature of someone or the underlying issue to a problem, brush your closed eyelids with fern before you meet the person, or start thinking about the issue.

THURSDAY

Thursday is the day of the gods Jupiter and Thor, both kings in their respective pantheons. Wear regal shades of blue and red and carry yourself with the confidence of knowing you have the protection of the deities. If you can afford it, donate to a charity or give food to a neighbor in need to gain the blessings of the Gods, as both Jupiter and Thor are protectors of the weak.

Thursday is the day for dealing with financial issues, so eat something that contains basil, a magic money herb. You could also keep a round-leafed green plant by the front door.

If you are having difficulties with overspending or being unable to save, take a large coin and a piece of long, thin, green ribbon. Wrap the ribbon around the coin until it is no longer visible, then make a knot on one side saying, "I make this knot, spend I will not." Next, make another knot on the other side, while saying: "Money comes to me, as I will it, so mote it be!" Keep the little knotted parcel somewhere safe and undisturbed until your goal is reached.

If you need extra magical energy for any spell you do this day, add an oak leaf or do the spell while sitting at an oaken table. The oak will lend its strength to your magic.

PRACTICAL MAGIC **FLOURISHING FINANCES**

Combine the mundane and magical management of money with this simple ritual to perform on a Thursday.

1 Make sure your front door is free of obstructions that could stop money energy coming into your home.

2 Call the elements by placing a coin in each elemental direction, then make a pentagram around it using more coins.

3 Say: "Money, money come to me. Financial opportunities with this ritual I'll see. I don't ask for much, just money for food, fun, and such!"

4 Then spend some time paying bills, checking your bank accounts for fraudulent activities, or looking for a side hustle.

5 When you are ready, move your coin pentagram under your doormat.

6 Thank the elements for the money they are bringing into the household.

FRIDAY

Friday is the day of the love goddess, Venus, so take the chance to do something you love today!

• Carry a rose quartz with you to send out some gentle and loving vibes to yourself and others.

• Wear pink or gentle reds, like burgundy.

• If you are seeking a relationship, mix a teaspoon of cinnamon with a pinch of ground red pepper. Dip your finger in the mixture and draw a heart on your forehead while saying: "Like a beacon will shine, this heart of mine, love I will find, this spell I hereby bind!" Repeat every Friday until you are in a steady relationship.

Because I love my pets, my nickname for this day is "Familiar Friday." All my pets get a treat and I spend more time with them. I also try to schedule adopting a new pet, or visits to the vet, for Friday where possible.

SATURDAY

This is the day of Saturn, known as the god of farming and food. It's a great day to do work in the garden as well as start projects that take a season, or even a year, to come to fruition (so definitely not "everyday magic" spells).

Saturn is also the god of protection, making Saturday a good day to get rid of negativity—especially when you want to stop someone from getting in your way. Wear black and gray clothes and understated jewelry on this day to soak up negativity. Use this day to clean your house and cleanse it magically at the same time! This can be as simple as smudging each room.

You can also try a simple cleansing ritual. Take a white candle (for peace and moving on) and draw an upward arrow on it in orange marker pen (orange is the color of justice, and the arrow is the rune symbolizing justice). Burn it and look into the flame, visualizing any negativity or obstacles being burned up in the fire and no longer being a problem.

SUNDAY

The day of the Sun God, Sunday is great for self-confidence magic, friendship spells, increasing power or male energy, and also business success.

Are you feeling too weak or powerless to deal with a problem? Perhaps you're not sure if a relationship is still good for you? Watch the sun come up on a Sunday and feel the sun's rays strengthen you, giving you the power to make a decision and stick by it.

CHAPTER 6

Seasonal Witchery

Witches often see seasonal witchery as "big magic," with major celebrations and long rituals for the Sabbats. But each season has its own magical energy, which you can harness as you go about your day, or as part of the traditions of the season.

Spring magic

Spring is the season of renewal and growth. That is why so many of us spring-clean our homes!

NATURE'S FRESH START

Spring is a great time to make a fresh start in your life, just like in the nature you see around you. Spend time outside watching the baby animals and fresh green plants all springing to life.

Green, along with gold, is the color of prosperity and wealth. If your lawn is patchy in places, reseed it to restore prettiness to your garden. This can also symbolize any debts or money issues being resolved. As you seed your lawn, chant the following words and think about growing in prosperity like the green grass:

A fresh start this spring I make,

For my happiness and contentment's sake!

Prosperity and wealth come to me,

For the good of all, so mote it be!

Give back to Mother Earth for the blessings you ask her for, and for sustaining you through the winter. Plant some wild grasses and flower seeds in a dirt spot on your way to work—you can say the same chant while doing this!

PRACTICAL MAGIC
FOUR ELEMENTS MEDITATION

Try this easy meditation that draws on the four elements to help you feel more balanced and grateful for all that you have in life.

1 Find a bit of vegetation to focus on—this could be a freshly potted plant on your windowsill, budding flowers in your garden, or fresh green leaves on a tree.

2 Think about how this bit of nature is being nurtured by the four elements. Earth brings it nutrients, air brings it oxygen, fire from the sun brings it warmth, and water in the form of rain helps it to grow.

3 Think about how you are part of nature too. Ask for Mother Earth to nourish your mind and body, for air to bring you inspiration, for fire to bring you passion, and for water to bring you intuition and wash away negativity.

4 When you feel relaxed and balanced, smile and thank the Earth Goddess for her blessings today and always.

SPRING BUNNIES

Bunnies are abundant in spring and are a symbol of fertility. With their brown coat and fluffy white tail, they represent the Earth Goddess. On your next walk, think of an issue or question and let any bunnies you encounter help you with a divination.

• If you spot two bunnies, this suggests you should take more responsibility in the situation that's on your mind.

• Three bunnies indicate that you should potentially be more passionate and energetic about the issue.

• If a bunny is calmly looking at you, take this as a sign that the issue you're worried about isn't that big a deal.

• A bunny hiding behind some yellow daffodils symbolizes that you should ask your friends for help (as yellow stands for friendship).

SPRING-CLEANING

Spring-cleaning shouldn't just be an annoying physical chore, but can be made into a magical exercise by following the tips below.

• Before or after you do the physical cleaning, walk around your home with a singing bowl. If you don't have one, simply fill a wine glass with some water and gently move your damp index finger around the rim of the glass to make it sing. The clear tone will help clear the house of lingering negativity and bad energy.

• As you clean, watch the dust being stirred up in the air and then falling to the ground or onto your duster. Visualize this as spiritual dust from a lazy winter being removed.

• Clean counterclockwise around your home to get rid of bad energies and intentions. Clean from the top of the room toward the floor, so any dust that falls will eventually be cleaned off the floor. As you clean, chant: "I am cleaning everything, removing clutter from the floor, until my mind with clarity will ring, whether a whisper or a roar!"

• Another useful magical chant while you sweep or mop is: "Sweep, sweep, sweep the ground, all negativity shall be bound, I banish all that is profane, only positives shall remain!"

• An aroma cleanse will deepen the magic of your spring-clean and make your home smell nice. Boil some water, add citrus peel, cinnamon for luck, peppermint for happiness, and a pinch of salt. As the water simmers, let the vapor rise and get into the nooks and crannies you can't reach.

• After cleaning, bless your home by lighting some pleasing incense, or sprinkling some rose water, walking clockwise around the home to increase blessings.

• Finally, take some time for yourself by having a snack. Something spring-related, like eggs or fresh spring greens, is a good choice.

BAY LEAF SPELL

As people start to go outside more in the spring, minds begin to naturally open up to new possibilities of friendship and love. To encourage these new connections, write an aim on a bay leaf, such as "finding new friends" or "looking for love."

Then, depending on the desired end result, do one of the following:

BURN IT for a quick if potentially messy result.

BURY IT to get a slow but strong result.

THROW IT TO THE WIND for inspiration and unusual results.

THROW IT INTO FLOWING WATER for an intense and deeply connected result.

PRACTICAL MAGIC
CAULIFLOWER DIVINATION

The white of a cauliflower symbolizes peace and pure energy. You can harness renewal and spring energy with this simple divination.

1 Cut a slice from the middle of a cauliflower on a sunny day, or at least in daylight.

2 Use it as a blank canvas to draw something that represents a new goal in your personal or professional life.

3 Keep the cauliflower slice on your altar or mantelpiece for a few days (discard it when it starts going bad).

4 At night, hold the rest of the cauliflower in both hands and chant nine times: "Lady Moon, come to me and bring me creativity. Lord of Sun, grant me energy so that the clear path I can see!"

5 Look at the plant and interpret any shapes in the whiteness for clues as to how to move forward with the goal you drew.

6 Use the cauliflower to make a meal. As you eat it, visualize your energy getting stronger and moving toward your goal.

Summer magic

The long, warm days of summer lend themselves to celebrations! Enjoy being outside and having fun in the sun with friends and family.

CELEBRATE SUMMER

Have a picnic in your garden or local park, or find a place that is overtly magical, like a holy spring, fairy fort, or a spot near an ancient megalithic site.

• If possible, try to eat produce grown locally to harness the local energy of the Earth Goddess and local spirits. Make fresh salads using locally grown fruits and vegetables. Add herbs from your garden or windowsill such as parsley, basil, thyme, chives, lavender, or peppermint.

• Summer is the Sun God's season, so eat yellow and orange foods that symbolize him, such as carrot slices, sweetcorn, mandarins or oranges, honeydew melon, and squash flowers.

• As it gets dark, you could light a bonfire. Jumping over it while staging a wish will help to make it come true.

• Take home some ashes from a bonfire attended with friends as this will help to keep friendships warm for all involved.

TREE VISUALIZATION

Find a big, healthy tree and stand with your back against it.

Visualize being grounded in the earth. Imagine the tree giving you the strength of the Earth Goddess and gaining the blessings of the Sun God through the branches reaching high into the sky.

Close your eyes for a few moments and inhale deeply while letting go of your mental burdens.

FRUITS OF THE SEASON

Going to pick summer berries is a nice reason to spend some quiet time with your love. And you can then harness the magical qualities of these fruits, too.

RASPBERRIES: To increase romantic love energies, make a raspberry bracelet or necklace (as pink is the color of romance). Find some firm, not overly ripe raspberries and push a needle with thread through each one from top to bottom. You can give it to your love, or wear it to draw love toward you. Eat the raspberries after talking to your love interest.

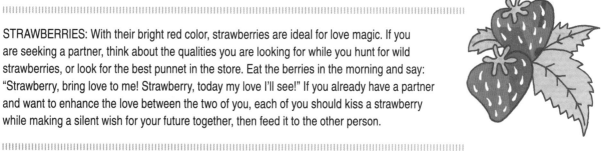

STRAWBERRIES: With their bright red color, strawberries are ideal for love magic. If you are seeking a partner, think about the qualities you are looking for while you hunt for wild strawberries, or look for the best punnet in the store. Eat the berries in the morning and say: "Strawberry, bring love to me! Strawberry, today my love I'll see!" If you already have a partner and want to enhance the love between the two of you, each of you should kiss a strawberry while making a silent wish for your future together, then feed it to the other person.

CHERRIES: If you want to stir passion within, choose cherries. For an easy spell to summon up more energy to achieve a goal, arrange five cherries into the shape of a pentagram. Place the cherries as the points and the stalks as the lines. Spend a few minutes looking at your cherry pentagram and thinking about what steps you need to take to reach your goal. Then, here's the best bit: eat the cherries.

BY THE WATER

Spending time near water during the hot summer months can help you cool down. But it's also a great place to spot animals, both above and below the water's surface.

Butterflies and dragonflies are full of magical symbolism. Both are seen in many cultures as the messengers of departed loved ones or spirits, so if you see one (especially if it seems to be following you), pay attention! Does it seem to lead you in a specific direction? Is it a particular color, and do you need to pay attention to the color's magical meaning? For example:

- **Green:** Watch your spending or try to find a way to make more money.

- **Blue:** Pay attention to your health.

- **Red:** Bring passion back into your life.

Perhaps it keeps trying to land on a specific part of your body to send you a message:

- **Left hand:** Pay more attention to your intuition about things.

- **Right hand:** Take action on a matter—don't wait any longer.

- **Head:** Think things through more thoroughly before taking action.

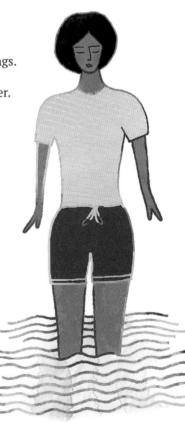

If you are out near fast-moving streams, you might see eels during the summer months. Eels are prominent shape-shifting symbols in Celtic mythology since the goddess Morrigan transformed into an eel when doing battle with Cú Chulainn. If you like shape-shifting meditations (where you visualize yourself as different animals), you could try looking at an eel or eating an eel dish before performing the meditation, to enhance its power.

LOOK FORWARD TO HARVEST

Summer won't last forever. Bring some magical summer energy into the following seasons by drying herbs and flowers in direct sunlight to harness the Sun God's energy. Keep them in a black cloth until ready to use in magic or magical cooking.

Of course, summer is also the time of wheat and other grain being ripe and being harvested. You can celebrate this time by making bread or a simple grain bowl. Alternatively, bring this symbol of abundance into your home by making small corn dollies with sweetcorn husks. They can be thrown on a fire with thanks to the Sun God for abundance and to Mother Nature for all the food we are blessed with this season.

Gather fragrant lavender flowers now. They can be collected from your garden, or they are often used as hardy groundcover near office complexes. They are a potent magical herb and can be used for relaxation before meditating and doing rituals, as well as for peace, friendship, and happiness spells.

PRACTICAL MAGIC **LAVENDER ICE CREAM**

If you have had a fight with a friend, or want to make peace with family, invite them over and make lavender ice cream, following the steps below. Alternatively, add some sprigs of lavender to a clear bottle of vodka and leave to infuse for a fortnight before giving it as a present.

1 Melt vanilla ice cream slightly.

2 Mix in lavender flowers and a few drops of lavender essential oil to taste.

3 Mix well and refreeze, then share it with the person with whom you want to make amends.

Autumn magic

Autumn is a colorful season, best known for the harvest and the turning of the leaves—from greens to fiery orange and red hues.

AUTUMN'S ABUNDANCE

Autumn is a joyous time and we reflect this by putting up decorations in yellow and orange, to ask the Sun God and warmth to stay a little longer, and gold, to symbolize the abundance that autumn brings.

You can meditate on abundance by taking a walk among the trees. Visualize the shedding of their colorful leaves as Mother Earth sharing her beauty with you.

If you eat meat, autumn is traditionally a time for hunting (in honor of the god Cernunnos) and making meat dishes, or drying or freezing it for abundance in future months. As you eat the meat, visualize the strength of a stag, the confidence of a boar, or the happiness of a sheep entering your body.

Witches will often decorate their altar and homes with apples around autumn, and use them for fortune-telling afterward (see page 56). But there are lots of autumnal vegetables and nuts that are useful for spellcasting, too, such as acorns, chestnuts, mushrooms, and pumpkins.

ACORNS

Great for decorating your altar or dinner table, acorns are very symbolic. Remember the saying "from tiny acorns, mighty oaks will grow."

• Keep acorns with any projects you have recently started to help them grow.

• Do a meditation to help your wishes come true—imagine planting an acorn and it growing into a strong oak under your care.

• Put an acorn in your wallet to help bring abundance and prosperity.

• For more potent money magic, draw an infinity symbol on some paper currency, sprinkle some cinnamon onto it, then fold the money around an acorn. Keep this with you at all times.

CHESTNUTS

This brown nut in its shell represents Mother Earth sleeping in winter, and the promise of energy and riches in the future. Chestnuts are good luck, too, and provide protection—they look like eyes, so they "look out for you."

If you need justice in a situation, cut a chestnut in two and rub the legal papers (or a photo of the other person involved, if it is not a legal issue) with one of the chestnut halves. Put the two halves back together with orange wax (the color of justice) and bury it westward of your home (for the healing power of the water element).

MUSHROOMS

Mushrooms symbolize the underworld and how thin the veil between the worlds is at this time of year. They make a particularly great snack before a meditation, fortune-telling, or an attempt to contact your ancestors.

Gather mushrooms in forest and field, but make sure you are certain about what you are picking; you don't want to get poisoned! Clean, chop, roast with some butter, and have on toast—the butter and golden toast symbolize the warmth and protection of the Sun God.

PUMPKINS

The pumpkin is an icon of autumn, symbolizing the abundance of food. Pumpkins have become more popular across Europe as visitors from the USA and Mexico, where the pumpkin is native, brought their own traditions there. In Native American mythology, pumpkins were grown by the three sisters —similar to the Celtic Maiden, Mother, and Crone goddesses.

Pumpkins were traditionally carved with scary shapes to scare away malevolent ghosts and negative energies. The candle inside represented the light of the God and Goddess, which burns negativity away. If you are having problems with gossipy neighbors, bullies walking home from school with your child, or an annoying roommate, carve a pumpkin!

See page 20 for more pumpkin magic.

A WALK IN THE WOODS

Leaves are great for decorating your altar or home, but they can also be used in simple magic and as an easy form of divination. Look to the ground during your woodland walks this season to see if a particular leaf catches your eye (see box, right).

AUTUMN LEAVES

Seek meaning from the autumn leaves around you:

OAK: Tells you to be strong about a current problem.

ALDER: Reminds you to be vigilant and protect yourself against spiritual attacks.

BROWN WITH YELLOW SPOTS: Symbolizes that friends (yellow) are important for the nourishment of the soul (brown), so make an effort to see your friends more often.

Use the colors of the leaves to decorate with purpose:

YELLOW: If you are hosting a party, decorate the table with yellow leaves to promote friendships.

RED: To increase passion, make a garland for your bedroom using red leaves.

PRACTICAL MAGIC **AUTUMN ALCHEMY**

Collect red leaves on your walk for this simple spell to quell discontent in your family. You will also need a blue candle, which represents healing.

1 Collect as many red leaves as there are members in your family.

2 Lay the leaves in a circle and place a blue candle in the middle.

3 Light the candle and visualize your family happy and content.

4 Say the following five times: "Red leaves, gift from earth, birth to death and death to birth. Keep all evil far away, day to night and night to day."

5 Blow out the candle and place one of the leaves in each family member's bedrooms, preferably under the bed or in the nightstand.

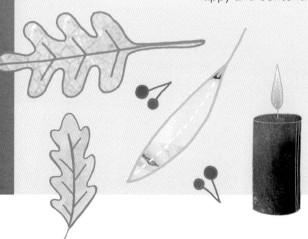

Winter magic

Many of us stay indoors during winter. This is part of our natural urge to stay warm. Winter is the season to slow down, restore, and grow spiritually during the long, dark nights.

WINTER WILDLIFE

It's important to stay connected to nature during the cold, dark months. Crisp winter days are perfect for dressing up warm and going for a walk to see some wildlife. Many animals are in hiding in the depths of winter, but you might still spot deer on your walks through the woods, or ducks in lakes and ponds.

STAG

The stag (male deer), with its magnificent antlers, is a symbol of all wild animals and their strength and natural beauty. It is also the symbol of the horned god, Cernunos, the god of the forest. If you spot one by chance, it is a sign that you should trust your own instinct and inner strength more. If you see two stags fighting, be reminded that there are many powers in your life, internal and external, and sometimes they clash, but things will get better (in the same way that the stags fight, but do not usually hurt each other).

DUCK

With their iridescent feathers shimmering in the sunlight, ducks are a symbol of the Sun God. Duck feathers can be used in magic to sweep away negative energy, so if you find a duck feather on your winter walks, keep it! You can use it to symbolically sweep your desk at work to move stress off, or a room after an argument, so no negative energy remains which could cloud later interactions in that room. Ducks also stand for honesty, so if you are having difficulty getting the truth out of someone, invite them for a walk by a duck pond to discuss things with them, or carry a duck feather while you speak to them.

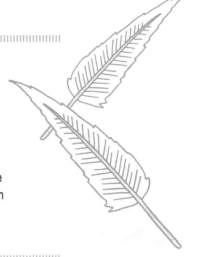

PRACTICAL MAGIC **UNWIND YOUR TROUBLES**

This easy winter walking ritual can help you find a solution to a problem.

1 Walk up a small hill in an upward spiral—a fairy fort (a hill where fairies are said to live) is best. As you walk, think of an issue you've been struggling with.

2 When you reach the top, drink something warming—tea or mulled wine in a flask. Visualize your troubles being carried away on the wind, and inspiration to solve your issue being carried to you by the breeze.

3 As you walk back down the hill, retrace your steps, slowly "unwinding" the spiral you formed when walking uphill.

PRACTICAL MAGIC **WINTER BANE**

Rid yourself of a bad habit or problem with this simple snow spell.

1 Make a small snow sculpture to represent your issue. This could be a cigarette shape if you are trying to give up smoking, a rectangle (to represent a computer monitor) if you spend too much time on your computer, or your neighbor's house number if you've been having problems with them.

2 As you create the sculpture, pour all your negative energy, such as fear or anger, into it.

3 Bring the snow sculpture inside and place it in your cauldron (or sink, if you don't have a cauldron).

4 Watch the snow melt, and as it disappears, visualize the bad habit lessening its power over you or the problem disappearing.

PRACTICAL MAGIC
UNFREEZE AND MOVE FORWARD

Change can be good, such as moving in with your partner, or bad, such as losing a job. A piece of ice shaped like a wand, particularly an icicle from outside your home, can help you accept changes happening in your life.

1 Face north, and draw a pentagram in the air with your ice wand, while saying: "Ice to earth, give me strength!"

2 Turn east, draw another pentagram, and say: "Ice to air, give me inspiration!"

3 Turn south, again draw a pentagram, and say: "Ice to fire, give me passion!"

4 Turn west, draw another pentagram, and say: "Ice to water, help me weather this change!"

5 Hold the ice wand to your forehead, mouth, and then heart.

6 Place it outside so it may refreeze or melt as the weather dictates.

WINTER BERRIES

Mistletoe is a traditional winter plant, and is also sacred to Druids, representing fertility (hence kissing under the mistletoe). In the old days, mistletoe was collected under a waxing moon and then fed to farm animals, to ensure healthy babies would be born in spring. Mistletoe is poisonous, so must not be eaten, but it is a popular Christmas decoration—go for a walk and forage for some to decorate your home with!

• Hang mistletoe over the doorway to draw love to you.

• Leave some under your bed if you want to conceive.

• Use a few small branches of mistletoe to make a circle around a symbol of something you want to draw abundance to—for example, around your ring light if you are a vlogger and want your social media channel to go viral, or around a coin to draw money to you.

Winter is also a good time to collect rose hips. Unsurprisingly, their strong red color represents passionate love. Share rose hip tea—sweetened with honey, stirred in clockwise—with your lover before a passionate night together. Alternatively, if you've been having trouble in your relationship and want to reignite the spark, place rose hips in the shape of a heart around a happy photo of you and your partner. As you do this, chant five times: "Love strong and true, I seek you. Whatever we now lack, we very much want it back!"

Conclusion:
Where to go from here

If you liked the everyday magic in this book, there are ways to go deeper and broaden your knowledge and skills so that you can continue your magic and worship exactly when and how you want.

First, you should explore by yourself, intellectually and spiritually, to learn what tradition of Wicca and what pantheon of deities works for you. Read a lot! There are some suggestions for other books on the next page. You can go online, too, to follow social media streams from witches of different traditions.

It's also great to meet other witches in person when you are ready. A good way to start mixing with other Wiccans is to meet with them socially at moots: these are witchy meetings that are held in pubs or community centers. At moots, there is usually a topic of the month which is discussed for an hour or so, and then everyone can mingle and chat. You can find listings of these on the websites of the main witchcraft organizations on page 140, or check the noticeboards of your local New Age, crystal, and health food stores.

You might find a study group in the same way, or even form one yourself. Groups usually meet monthly, somewhere like a coffee shop, to discuss a witchy book, a mythological story, or a particular type of magic (such as candle spells, gemstone magic, or thanksgiving rituals). Such meetings give everyone in the group the freedom to practice how they want, rather than according to ideas and traditions that may not suit the individual exactly, but still enables each witch to learn from one another.

After meeting other witches a few times, you may be invited to celebrate the main Sabbats with others in a semi-public gathering, and from there, an invite to a coven might follow.

FURTHER READING

If you liked this book, you might also like some of my other books:

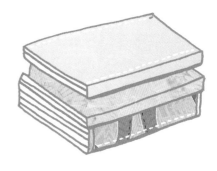

• *Seasons of the Witch* (CICO Books, 2025), a guide to celebrating major and minor Sabbats, as well as other significant dates in the Wiccan year.

• *The Green Wiccan Spell Book* (CICO Books, 2019), a compendium of magical knowledge.

• *The Green Wiccan Year* (CICO Books, 2018), a planner which includes magical tips.

• *The Green Wiccan Herbal* (CICO Books, 2016), a guide to 52 magical herbs plus spells and rituals.

I would also recommend books by Kate West:

• *The Real Witches' Book of Spells and Rituals* (Element Books, 2003)

• *The Real Witches' Kitchen* (Thorsons, 2002)

• *The Real Witches' Handbook* (Thorsons, 2001)

And this one by Cerridwen Greenleaf:

• *The Book of Kitchen Witchery* (CICO Books, 2016)

For a more traditional approach, check out Scott Cunningham's book:

• *Cunningham's Encyclopedia of Magical Herbs* (Llewellyn, 1985)

USEFUL ORGANIZATIONS AND WEBSITES

www.atcwicca.org
The Aquarian Tabernacle Church has a great American Wiccan website.

www.circlesanctuary.org
Circle Sanctuary: author and famous Wiccan Selena Fox's website and organization with information on life rituals, events, interfaith work, and more.

www.cog.org
Covenant of the Goddess: this mostly US-based group works on getting legal recognition for Wicca and is very active in networking.

www.druidry.org
Order of Bards, Ovates, and Druids: a UK-based but worldwide community of people who practice Druidry, a spiritual philosophy that connects people with nature.

www.facebook.com/SiljasGreenWiccan
My Facebook page, regularly updated with news and other links of interest.

www.learnreligions.com/ paganism-wicca-4684806
This website has great, unbiased info on Wicca.

www.paganfed.org
The Pagan Federation: a UK-based, international organization that runs witchy events and also has a great magazine.

www.patheos.com/pagan
Excellent Pagan blog with rituals, music suggestions, and insights into day-to-day Pagan living.

www.sacred-texts.com
Religious and spiritual texts, including Wiccan, Druid, and ancient Shaman.

www.thealmanack.com
A calendar-style website with current moon phases, planets that rule the day, etc. Has a handy monthly printable page.

www.witchcraft.org
Children of Artemis: a UK-based organization with an informative website. They also run witchy gatherings and conventions, and publish a magazine.

Glossary

Altar A witch's personal sacred space, usually in their home, where magical tools are kept.

Cauldron A large pot or bowl, traditionally black, used to make magical foods and for water-scrying.

Chakras The main points of energy in the body. Includes the crown chakra (top of the head) and the third eye chakra (on the forehead between the eyebrows).

Cleansing Spiritual cleaning, removing negativity.

Coven A group of witches working magic together regularly.

Deity A god or goddess.

Deosil Clockwise direction.

Divination Reading the future with tarot cards, runes, or other methods.

Dowsing Finding energy lines or water lines by holding an L-shaped branch that will point downward when a line is present.

Elements Each of the four elements are linked to particular colors and directions—earth: brown/green, north; air: yellow/white, east; fire: red/orange, south; water: blue, west. This is often symbolized during rituals by using candles in those colors placed in the corresponding positions.

Familiar Animal, often a pet, who helps in magic.

Gods and Goddesses There are many gods and goddesses in mythology, but there is also the concept of God for male energy/all male deities and Goddess for female energy/all female deities/goddess power in women.

Grounding Releasing excess energy after magic.

Lord and Lady Alternative terms for God and Goddess.

Pantheon A group of deities associated with a particular culture, such as the Celtic pantheon or Greek pantheon.

Patron deity Like a more powerful guardian angel, this is a god or goddess you feel especially close to at this time in your life.

Pentagram A five-pointed star without a circle, although the term is often used interchangeably with pentacle (a five-pointed star in a circle).

Psychic A person who is extremely sensitive to energies and otherwordly entities.

Rede/Wiccan Rede The basic Wiccan moral standpoint: "And it harm none, do as thou wilt."

Runes Ancient angular letters/symbols that can be used for divination and other magic.

Sabbat A major Wiccan festival—there are eight Sabbats each year.

Scrying Form of divination done by looking in a pool of water, crystal ball, mirror, etc.

Sigil A magical symbol, often personally designed.

Smudging A method of spiritual cleansing to remove negativity, performed by burning herbs (often sage) and allowing the smoke to waft through areas and over items in need of cleansing.

Talisman A magical amulet.

Visualization Imagining something in your mind's eye. Also used for very deep meditation.

Warding Protecting something magically.

Widdershins Counterclockwise.

Index

Acknowledgments

There are so many people who have aided me on my spiritual path that I would like to acknowledge—from the more obvious, like my family and my hippy parents who let me do my own thing, through my fellow students at Trinity College way back in the Fortean Society, where we explored all kinds of spiritual phenomena, to all the friends who became coven members over the years. I may have run a training coven, but I learned a lot from them, too!

And there were non-humans too, like my familiar Piggy (a tuxedo cat—never found another one as magical), the deer I see when walking the dog (who always seem to have some wisdom to impart that I need to intuit) and, of course, the dogs that have come and gone throughout my life.

Most of all, I would like to thank Anthony Kemp, whose spiritual name, Robin, led to my first girl being named Robyn, and who has been instrumental in my Wiccan path. He passed into the next world many years ago, but I still miss him.